Help me, I'm buying a house!

A practical guide for buying your own home in England and Wales.

From First Time Buyers, for First Time Buyers and those who don't know what they are doing.

By Sandra Starke, PhD

with Dan Boddice, PhD

With illustrations

by

Ben Jones

Dedicated to all of you who are trying to get onto the property ladder despite the adversities. You will make it!

Contents

Chapter 1

What you should consider right now.

1. WHAT YOU SHOULD CONSIDER RIGHT NOW

This chapter looks at things that you may want to consider doing right now, even if buying a property is still a distant fantasy. It can be important to make certain provisions early (many months and even years in advance) in order to fully benefit from financial support schemes and being able to move without being stuck for example in a rental contract. In this chapter, we hence take a look at the following:

- Saving through a Help to Buy ISA or Lifetime ISA and the associated 25% government top-up (free money!).

- Tenancy agreements and how to get out of them.

- Connecting with stakeholders such as new build developers and banks/building societies.

- Building up your credit history.

Chapter 1 contents

1.1 Help to buy ISA

We thought the best way to start this book is to boost your funds. Hence, drum-roll for the Help to Buy ISA! This is a scheme for all first time buyers that is offered by most banks. The basic conditions (a 25% bonus on savings for a property purchase) are identical, but some banks might give you some extra interest for having the money in the account. As you will find out later in the book, the definition of a 'first time buyer' varies depending on what you are trying to do. To qualify for a help to buy ISA:

- You cannot ever have had interest in any property: if you don't own and have never owned any bit of any property anywhere, bought or inherited, you are good. If you inherited 1/16th of a house that you since sold, you can't have the Help to Buy ISA. This goes for properties both inside and outside the UK.

- You have to be a UK resident.

- You have to be aged 16 and over.

- You need a valid National Insurance number (that seems to be new).

- You can't have another active cash ISA in the same tax year. If you have an active ISA already, you can still open a Help to Buy ISA but this requires a few additional steps to swap it.

Qualify? Read on!

1.1.1 What is a Help to Buy ISA and what do you get?

The Help to Buy ISA is a government-run scheme that will give you 25% tax-free extra money on your savings specifically for the deposit for your home purchase. The deposit is what you pay at completion (when all the money shuffles across to the vendor and you get the keys), not the 10% you pay to the solicitor at the exchange of contracts earlier in the process. This means that when you are ready to get the keys and put the full deposit down, the government will give you a quarter of what you saved up in this account, extra, for free.

The Help to Buy ISA supports purchases up to the value of £250,000 outside of London, respectively up to £450,000 in London. If you want to buy a more expensive property, you won't get the free cash.

You can open the account at any time – the earlier you open it, the more you get. This is how it works:

- When opening the account, you can **deposit up to £1,200**. That could be an immediate free £300 that you will receive later on, as long as you save a minimum total of £1,600 in the account.

- You are then allowed to save **up to £200 every month**. That means that every month, you get another free £50. Be aware that if you don't put the money down in a given month, you can't put down twice as much in the next. It's up to £200 per month; the rest is 'gone'.

- You might have to sort out your current ISA. The bank will help you with that, just ask.

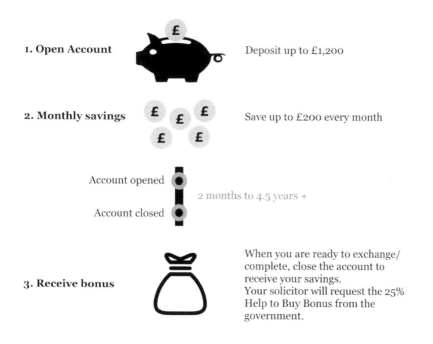

1. Open Account Deposit up to £1,200

2. Monthly savings Save up to £200 every month

Account opened
2 months to 4.5 years +
Account closed

3. Receive bonus When you are ready to exchange/ complete, close the account to receive your savings. Your solicitor will request the 25% Help to Buy Bonus from the government.

Figure 1. Help to Buy ISA illustrated.

The way this works out is easy to see: if you open the account early, you get more money. The maximum amount you get, however, is £3,000. If you put in £1,200 at the start and £200 every month after, that would mean you maximise your gains if you start saving 4 ½ years before you get the keys to your home.

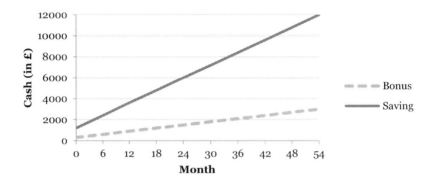

Figure 2. Increase in your savings and 25% bonus over time if you put the maximum amount into your Help to Buy ISA every month - £1,200 when you open it, then £200 monthly. When you complete your purchase and transfer the funds through your solicitor, you receive a 25% government bonus on everything you have saved up to that point.

The scheme is guaranteed until 2030, by which time you will have to use it. There is also news that after 20 November 2019, you cannot open a new account anymore. Check for updates on this.

1.1.2 Buying together

If you buy together with someone else, BOTH of you can have a Help to Buy ISA, as long as both of you qualify as a first time buyer. So you double the amount of free money you get! If only one of you qualifies as a first time buyer, only that person can have the account. But you can still buy together, and this person will still get the bonus.

1.1.3 How to cash the bonus

When you are ready to close the account to use the funds towards the full deposit on your purchase, your solicitor will have to get the bonus for you. Your solicitor will basically have to manage the process of closing the account, transfer of funds including the bonus and organising a small amount of paperwork. This usually comes at a fee – they are allowed to charge up to £60 inclusive of VAT (and oh yes, they will milk it). Make sure your solicitor does this between exchange and completion.

You will only receive the bonus on COMPLETION – that's when you pay for the house and get the keys. Hence, you cannot use it towards the initial deposit which you have to hand over to the solicitor before exchange of contracts, usually 10% of the purchase price. You might hence have to manage a cash-flow issue.

The government website gives the following advice:

> *"When you are close to buying your first home, you will need to instruct your solicitor or conveyancer to apply for your government bonus. Once they receive the government bonus, it will be added to the money you are putting towards your first home. The bonus must be included with the funds consolidated at the completion of the property transaction. The bonus cannot be used for the deposit due at the exchange of contracts, to pay for solicitor's, estate agent's fees or any other indirect costs associated with buying a home."*

https://www.helptobuy.gov.uk/help-to-buy-isa/how-does-it-work/

1.1.4 What if you don't end up buying?

If you don't end up buying a property or need the money for something else, you can take it out of the account. You just won't get the 25% bonus.

1.1.5 More info

- Information on the Help to Buy ISA scheme can be found here:

  https://www.helptobuy.gov.uk/help-to-buy-isa/how-does-it-work/

  and here:

  https://www.gov.uk/affordable-home-ownership-schemes/help-to-buy-isa

- Further advice on the scheme can be found here, which is also nicely explained:

  https://www.moneysavingexpert.com/savings/help-to-buy-ISA/

1.1.6 Who can help?

If you need direct help, speak to a Help to Buy ISA advisor or other customer advisor that you will find in all major banks in the UK. You may have to book an appointment, or you can just pop in. It will be easy.

1.2 Lifetime ISA (LISA)

Lifetime ISA and Help to Buy ISA have many similarities; however have a look at this section to understand the main differences. Getting the choice between the two right can make a big difference.

1.2.1 What is a Lifetime ISA and what do you get?

The Lifetime ISA was introduced in April 2017. You can use it for TWO purposes:

- Towards your first home if you are a first time buyer.

- Towards your retirement after you are 60.

If you want to use it towards your retirement, read up on it online, as there are lots of things you should inform yourself about in comparison to a pension and regarding penalties of early money withdrawal. For example, have a look here: https://www.gov.uk/lifetime-isa.

If you want to use it towards your first home, read on.

In summary, the LISA:

- Lets you save more every year.

- Pays the bonus into the account at the end of every year, so you get interest on it.

- Has a penalty if you take money out early – you lose 6% of what you take out, as you pay a 25% penalty on your savings including the bonus.

- Lets you get a higher bonus if you save for many years.

- Lets you buy a more expensive house.

- Can't be used towards your own first property in the first 12 months – you have to wait at least 12 months after opening the account before you can get the bonus.

The LISA for first time buyers works similarly to the Help to Buy ISA: it will give you 25% tax-free extra on your savings specifically for your home purchase. However, there are differences between the two ISAs, which are best summarised in a table:

Table 1. Comparison between Help to Buy ISA and Lifetime ISA.

	Help to Buy ISA	Lifetime ISA
Maximum saving per year	£2,400 (£3,600 in first year)	£4,000
How long until you can get 25%?	3 months	12 months
Maximum property price	£250,000*	£450,000
Saving style	Up to £200/month; plus £1,200 in first month	Both, monthly savings or lump sums, OK
Penalty in case of withdrawal for other purpose	No	Yes
Maximum overall bonus	£3,000	£32,000**
Maximum bonus after 6 months	£550	£0
Maximum bonus after 1 yr	£900	£1,000
Maximum bonus after 2 yrs	£1,500	£2,000
Maximum bonus after 3 yrs	£2,100	£3,000
Minimum age	16	18
Maximum age	None	39

*excluding London, where it's £450,000

**after 32 years of saving

The LISA works a bit easier than the Help to Buy ISA in that you can put lump sums in, so you don't have to save exactly £200 every month. With the LISA, you can put in £4,000 at the start of every year or put in smaller amounts throughout the year, it doesn't matter.

Bear in mind that, still, not many banks offer LISAs. Have a look online at your options.

1.2.2 Buying together

The same rules apply as for the Help to Buy ISA.

1.2.3 How to cash the bonus

This works the same as for the Help to Buy ISA. The government website (https://www.gov.uk/lifetime-isa) provides the following rules:

- You buy the property at least 12 months after you open the Lifetime ISA.

- You use a conveyancer or solicitor to act for you in the purchase - the ISA provider will pay the funds directly to them.

- You're buying with a mortgage.

1.2.4 What if you don't end up buying

If you don't end up buying a property, you can simply keep the LISA open and use it towards retirement after you hit age 60. Otherwise, if you take the money out, you will pay a penalty. However, before you use it for your pension, have a look at the pros and cons, as there are better ways to build up a pension.

If you take money out of the account, you pay a 25% penalty. This sounds as if you just break even. However, say you take all the money out, you can see that in fact you are losing around 6% of your savings, since the penalty is on your savings INCLUDING the bonus, which is paid to you annually. An example:

- You paid in 12,000 over 3 years.

- Your **25% bonus of £3,000** is already added on top, since you get the bonus into the account at the end of every year.

- You hence have £15,000 in your account.

- You pay a 25% penalty on the full £15,000.

- Your **penalty is £3,750.**

- You hence can only retrieve £11,250 of your 'own' money that you put in and lose £750.

Whether or not someone in government didn't do the maths right when coming up with the penalty is subject to speculation. Fact is it will bite you in the bum.

1.2.5 More info

- More information on the Lifetime ISA can be found on the government website here:

  https://www.gov.uk/lifetime-isa

- A comparison between Help to Buy ISA and Lifetime ISA can be found here:

  https://blog.moneysavingexpert.com/2016/04/the-help-to-buy-isa-v-lifetime-isa-which-should-first-time-buyers-get/

- General advice on the Lifetime ISA can also be found here:

  https://www.moneysavingexpert.com/savings/lifetime-ISAs/

1.2.6 Who can help

Speak to your bank, building society, mortgage broker or independent financial advisor for help.

1.3 Tenancy agreement

Getting out of your tenancy is an important prerequisite when you want to buy your own place. Be aware that in a worst-case scenario where you are stuck in a fixed-term rental contract, you will have to pay off the full rent until the end of your fixed term contract. This applies even if you move out before the end of it. Hence, plan ahead and have a look at the options below.

1.3.1 Rolling tenancy agreement

Once you know that you want to buy your own place, you have to get ready to get out of any current rental agreements – unless you live with your parents, which makes the whole situation easier to manage.

If you live in rented accommodation, the easiest way to manage this is to move onto a rolling contract ('periodic tenancy'). You can do that at the point of contract renewal – ask to move onto a rolling contract, which should give you a **1-month notice period**. If you need to move rental property, try to get a contract with a short, fixed-term duration and then move onto a rolling contract. Most agents usually try to talk you out of it, since they get extra fees every time you renew a fixed term contract. Don't let that distract you. The only risk is that of course a rolling contract is less secure than a fixed-term one – while nothing can happen to you and your rent on a fixed term contract, your landlord can serve notice on a rolling one. In theory, rent increases should still only be possible once a year, but do check. If you go on a rolling contract, find out what the notice period for the landlord is. These are risks to weigh up.

Remember that to end a rolling contract, you need to give notice. This is somewhat different from the end of a fixed term contract. Your contract might have the clause that your fixed term contract automatically moves on to a roiling contract if neither party gives notice. In this case, you will have to give notice as well. Check your contract, as your agent might give you incorrect information. Always go back to the paperwork.

Finally, being on a rolling contract with a 1-month notice period makes you a very desirable buyer, and when bidding for a property, it might tip the balance in your favour. Even if you offer a few thousand less compared to someone who has to sell their house or is otherwise stuck with obligations, the much reduced hassle might mean that your offer will be accepted. Definitely point this out when making your bid (see Chapter 5.2 and 6.4).

1.3.2 Getting out of a fixed term tenancy contract early

This might be tricky. First of all, check your contract for a break clause. You can negotiate that when signing the contract. Chances are there is none.

Second, you can ask your landlord to leave early, termed 'surrender the tenancy' or asking for 'early release'. This most likely will have to go through the agent. If you can support finding a new tenant or already have found a replacement for yourself, this might improve your chances of getting out of the contract.

Third, you can try to negotiate leaving early and paying part of the remaining rent. Chances are your landlord will find someone new and might make a nice little bonus for themselves.

Make sure that whatever you agree, it is in writing and dated.

1.3.3 More info

- Advice from the Citizen's Advice Bureau on ending your tenancy can be found here:

   https://www.citizensadvice.org.uk/housing/renting-privately/ending-your-tenancy/ending-your-tenancy/

- Further advice on ending your tenancy can be found on the government website here:

   https://www.gov.uk/private-renting-tenancy-agreements/how-to-end-your-tenancy

- Finally, Shelter also offers good advice on ending your tenancy:

   https://england.shelter.org.uk/housing_advice/private_renting/how_tenants_can_end_a_fixed_term_tenancy

1.3.4 Who can help?

If you need direct help, contact your local Citizens Advice Bureau:

https://www.citizensadvice.org.uk

Be aware that there may be a wait time of a week or more. If there is an urgent issue, go there in person for the morning slots.

If you have a problem with a letting agent that warrants a complaint, you can contact Propertymark:

http://www.propertymark.co.uk/complaints/

Many agents are member of ARLA or other bodies and have to abide by their standards. Propertymark may also be able to help with other letting agent related issues which you are unable to resolve.

1.4 Get on mailing lists for new builds

If you are thinking about buying a new build, it is a good idea to get onto their mailing lists early. Typically, developers release information about new sites very early, and the sooner the know, the easier it is to get a good plot. You can also periodically check their websites. Information is typically released in the following order:

- Where are they going to develop next

- When will they start selling plots

- Which plots they have for sale at which price

If you are the first one to choose, you'll get the best plot, it's as simple as that. Early on you simply buy 'off plan' based on images. Later on, there will already be a show home and/or homes that are already partially or fully built. Some developers don't sell off plan until they have the first show home up. Reservation fees are typically not astronomical (around £1000 to £2000 and maybe reduced for first time buyers), so as long as you are prepared to put up with a potentially massively uncertain timeline, the early bird catches the worm. 'Massively uncertain timeline' means that the date on which your home should be done and ready to move into might shift by 6 to 12 months.

For a list of property developers, have a look for example here:

https://www.whathouse.com/housebuilders/

Amongst the most well known developers are Barratt Homes, David Wilson Homes, Hill, St Modwen Homes, Kier Living, William Davis, Taylor Wimpey and Redrow Homes. There are many more developers, including regional ones and smaller companies. The quality and customer service of all of these developers vary, so do make sure to do your research. Take a look at Chapter 3. , Section 3.5.4 for more advice on new builds.

1.5 Get a credit card and regularly repay it

This may come as a surprise, but not needing a credit card does not put you in a good position to get a mortgage: there will be no history of you paying back any money that you borrow, and hence you are considered a risk. How would the bank know that you will pay them back if you have never shown that you pay anyone else back?

If you don't already have a credit card, get one. You can spend a certain amount of money with it every month and immediately repay it (it is advisory to not build up debt obviously). You can even set up an automatic payment of your credit card bills from your current account. The upshot of a credit card is also that your purchases are better protected. For example, an expensive flight when the airline goes bust will be refunded easily. Further, you might get a nifty little deal when opening a credit card, such as a voucher, free insurance or other perks. Make sure you get one with a low interest rate (APR) and ideally one that lets you make free withdrawals abroad. Remember that each time you get a credit card, it will leave a footprint on your credit file. Getting one the month before you make a mortgage application might not be the smartest move.

If you already have a credit card, act as above: build up a history of reliable lending repayments.

1.6 Get with your favourite bank or building society

This will sound weird. What this means is: have a look at mortgage rates and conditions already. If you find a lender that you really like the look of, open a current account with them. This will build up your track record and may even get you preferential rates or cashback after a few months with them. Also, if you want to open a Help to Buy ISA, you could do it with them. Don't forget to check out a building society starting with 'Nation' and ending with 'Wide', who in the past have had some of the most competitive mortgage rates and deals for First Time Buyers. The benefit of a building society is that their main business comes from good mortgages. Regular banks are calibrated a bit differently.

Chapter 2

Constraints

2. CONSTRAINTS

This chapter looks at constraints that are worth considering when planning what property and mortgage to go for. When looking at the costs of buying and running your own home, there are several things that all stack up, both at the point of purchase and after moving in. In this chapter, we systematically go through these to help you develop a better idea of your own scenario. We look at:

- Costs involved in buying a house – it's not just the property price, you have to factor in additional costs that require savings, such as stamp duty, solicitor fees and repairs.

- Having a look at affordability in context of what kind of mortgage people may get based on their circumstances.

- Running costs for your own home, including both the 'normal' costs and new costs that you get when you own a property.

- In context of the buying and running costs, information to help approximate the rough monthly repayments that may be realistic.

- Finally, a quick look at whether it is – after all – worth buying your own home.

Chapter 2 contents

2.1 Costs involved in buying a house

It is important to realise that the cost of the property is not the only cost which you have to plan and budget for when buying. This section provides a breakdown of most of the costs you might encounter on the way. Before we go into the details, the table below provides a summary of expected costs and their necessity. It highlights that you are unlikely to get away with less than £5000 in costs for the whole process, and you may want to budget for £10,000 if you have repairs and stamp duty to pay. Remember, even if you knock money off the cost of the house in any negotiation, you will still have to find the cash for repairs from your savings.

Table 2. Summary of (potential) costs involved in buying a property.

Item	Approx. cost	Requirement
Stamp duty (First Time Buyer)*	£0	Never owned any property
Stamp duty (lower rate)**	£2,500	Buy and sell at the same time
Stamp duty (higher rate)**	£10,000	Own more than one property
Solicitor	£1,200	YES
Survey	£600	Recommended
Mortgage arrangement fee	£1,000	NO
Mortgage booking fee	£200	NO
Broker fees	£500	NO
Valuation fee	£300	NO
Outstanding rent (one month if you are lucky)	£750	YES
Moving	£300	YES
Basic furniture	£600	YES
Repairs	£2000	YES
Total including everything	£17,450	
Total for standard costs	**£5,450**	

*Up to £300,000 purchase

**For illustration on 250,000k purchase

2.1.1 Stamp duty

Stamp Duty Land Tax (SDLT) applies to property purchases in England and Northern Ireland. Scotland and Wales have a slightly different system.

You pay stamp duty on completion of the house purchase. There are different rates depending on your circumstances, and this can make all the difference. This section concentrates on rates for residential dwellings bought as freehold. If you are buying a leasehold, please use an online stamp duty calculator to estimate your tax.

First time buyer (same across UK)

Based on the definition of a first time buyer given in the previous chapter (never had any 'interest' in any property anywhere), you don't have to pay stamp duty at all on house prices up to £300,000, and you get a reduced rate for house prices between £300,000 and £500,000. These figures are the same for London. This is the best position to be in. For a £250,000 house, your stamp duty would be £0.

If you bought a home before

If you are moving home from a place that you already bought, you pay a 'lower rate' stamp duty. If you are not buying and selling on the same day, you can request a refund if you sell your previous home within 3 years – but make sure you have the funds to pay for the required amount in the meantime.

England (and Northern Ireland)

In England, if you are moving home and selling your previous main residence at the same time, for a £250,000 house, your stamp duty would be £2,500. You can use the tax calculator here:

https://www.tax.service.gov.uk/calculate-stamp-duty-land-tax/#/intro.

If you keep hold of your previous home and hence own more than one home, you have to pay an extra 3% on the rates in the stamp duty table. That means that for a £250,000 house, your stamp duty would be £10,000.

Table 3. Stamp Duty Land Tax (SDLT) for freehold purchases in England and Northern Ireland.

Property or lease premium or transfer value	SDLT rate
Up to £125,000	0%
The next £125,000 (the portion from £125,001 to £250,000)	2%
The next £675,000 (the portion from £250,001 to £925,000)	5%
The next £575,000 (the portion from £925,001 to £1.5 million)	10%
The remaining amount (the portion above £1.5 million)	12%

Wales

Wales has the Land Transaction Tax (LTT), which is given in the table below. You can use the tax calculator here:

https://beta.gov.wales/land-transaction-tax-calculator.

As in England, if you keep hold of your previous home and hence own more than one home, you have to pay an extra 3% on the rates in the stamp duty table.

Table 4. Land Transaction Tax (LTT) for freehold purchase in Wales.

Purchase Price	LTT rate
The portion up to and including £180,000	0%
The portion over £180,000 up to and including £250,000	3.5%
The portion over £250,000 up to and including £400,000	5%
The portion over £400,000 up to and including £750,000	7.5%
The portion over £750,000 up to and including £1,500,000	10%
The portion over £1,500,000	12%

2.1.2 Solicitor / Conveyancing

Conveyancing is the legal process accompanying your purchase that transfer s home ownership to you. As all legal activities, it costs a lot. While prices in the London area are generally higher, be aware that you can use any solicitor or conveyance anywhere to work for you – they do not have to be local. In fact, those offered by agents or some banks are often based halfway across the country. It's hard to find a good solicitor, so ask around – a good solicitor is worth a lot more than a local one.

Depending on the property value, solicitor location and qualifications, a solicitor may cost between £1,000 and £3,000.

2.1.3 Survey

Even if your bank carries out a valuation (see below), you should carry out your own survey. The valuation conducted by the bank is very superficial, does not look beyond items that would basically result in the house falling down and you won't get to see the report. Word of mouth has is that the lender might sometimes even just drive past to check the property is actually there. Unless you conduct a survey, you will buy a house in a more or less unknown state apart from things that are obvious to your eyes. A survey will also enable you to re-negotiate the property price should significant issues come up that you were not aware of when making the offer.

Depending on the type of survey, it can cost anything from around £300 to £800+. Read more about surveys in Chapter 3.3.

2.1.4 Mortgage, broker and other fees

1. Mortgage arrangement fee

You will find that when deciding on a mortgage, you typically have two options: a slightly lower rate with an arrangement fee, or a slightly higher rate without an arrangement fee. Typically, in the long run, there is not much of a difference between the two options. The arrangement fee is usually in the region of £1000 to £2000. If you go for this option, make sure you have the funds. Alternatively, you can often add the fee to the loan. Also make sure that you don't have to pay the fees if your purchase does not complete.

2. Mortgage booking fee

Some banks might charge you a booking fee at the point of application. This is non-refundable and might cost around £200.

3. Broker fees

There are many brokers around that offer supporting you throughout the home buying process. Some are independent, others are based at estate agents. Depending on their services, they may charge £500 to £1,000 for helping you through the process. You might not need this at all – for example, you can shop around for mortgages yourself and can take over a lot of chasing. If you can get a free appointment, it's always a good starting point for someone unfamiliar with the buying process though. If you do arrange a mortgage through a broker, then you have to pay the additional broker fee above (£500 to £1000). Make sure it is worth it.

4. Valuation fee

Depending on the bank you want to have the mortgage from and your circumstances, you might be charged a valuation fee for the home you choose. All banks will value the property which they are lending on, although some do not charge for this. If they do charge, it might cost up to around £400. You pay this at the point of mortgage application and will not get it refunded if the purchase does not go through. Ask your lender about this when first comparing mortgages.

2.1.5 Other costs

1. Outstanding rent

When calculating costs, factor in outstanding rent that will likely have to be paid during the transition period where you move into your new home but are still in a rental agreement. In the best case scenario, this will be the rent for one month, so around £450 to £900. If your new home needs repairs and you anticipate a period where you are staying in rented accommodation while sorting things out, or if you are stuck in a fixed term contract, this can easily run into the thousands. Make sure that your salary and/or savings are sufficient to cover these costs on top of any mortgage and insurance payments. You might also have to pay twice the council tax, although if one property is unoccupied, council tax may not be chargeable. Check with your council. Also note that your home (buildings- and contents-) insurance will not allow you to leave your new home unoccupied for more than 1-2 months in a row depending on the policy. Again, find out early. If you need to leave the property unoccupied for longer, make sure that your insurance covers this.

2. Moving

Have a think what it will cost for you to move:

- Rental van (book early, ideally on a weekday where it is cheaper and there are less cars in the road, although you need to take time off work).

- Do you need porters?

- Do you need cleaners?

- What obligations do you have for handing over your rental property?

- Any works that you want to do before moving in, like carpet cleaning, paining, fixing small issues etc.

If things are reasonably easy, moving might cost you around £300. If you have a grand piano, 2 children, tons of furniture and a 4-bedroom house, you might be looking at closer to £1,000-£2,000.

3. Basic furniture

You need somewhere to sleep, eat, sit and put your stuff. If you are on a tight budget, there are many cheap options like Gumtree, Freecycle or local charity shops. However, be aware that you run the risk of introducing problems – especially with bedroom items, you really don't want to pick up bed bugs. With living room items, you don't want a flea infested couch. So be sensible.

We all know a Swedish budget furniture store, where you should be able to make a sound start on a budget of around £600. This might be a workable way to go, unless you have more funds for furniture. For a similar budget, Argos also offers loads of furniture, with the added bonus of free delivery over a certain cost of goods.

2.1.6 What else to budget for

1. Electrical and heating assessment

If you are buying an older property with no track record of electrics, you probably want to have the 'wiring' checked out. A re-write of a property costs around £3,000, so this is a big ticket item. The NICEIC is the body through which you can find a certified electrician:

https://www.niceic.com/householder/find-a-contractor

An extensive check that takes a lot of the day will cost you around £150.

While you are at it, you might also want to have the gas central heating checked out. This is a quicker job and may cost around £60. You can find certified personnel via the gas safety register:

https://www.gassaferegister.co.uk/.

2. Repairs

If you buy your own home, you have to budget for repairs. These might be smaller things that came up on the survey, something suddenly breaking or other expected or unexpected costs. Remember that with a 'used' home, you won't have any warranties once you got the keys, unless any warranties have been transferred to you (for example for roof repairs, window installations etc.). On a new build, you get a 10-year warranty, so you can budget less for repairs which would be paid for by the developer or warranty scheme. When buying an older house, you probably want to budget for a safety net of around £2000, which should cover roof works or a new boiler. Also make sure to check what items your buildings insurance covers and what the excess, conditions and exemptions are.

3. New running costs

Your own home will come with a few new additional costs compared to renting, which the next chapter will take a closer look at. However, as a basic guidance, you will have to budget for:

- Building insurance.
- Contents insurance.
- Life and critical illness insurance.
- Other potential insurances such as mortgage indemnity guarantee or repayment cover.
- Service charge (flats and some new builds).
- Parking charge (less common).

So you might need another £100 to £300 extra each month to cover this.

2.1.7 More info

- Information on stamp duty in England, Northern Ireland and general info can be found on the government website here:

https://www.gov.uk/stamp-duty-land_tax

- The equivalent information for Wales can be found on the government website here:

  https://gov.wales/funding/fiscal-reform/welsh-taxes/land-transaction-tax/?lang=en

- General advice on stamp duty can also be found here:

  https://www.moneysavingexpert.com/mortgages/mortgage-fees-stamp-duty/

2.2 What property price can I afford?

That is the big question. The bottom line is: no matter how big your budget, you will just about not be able to afford your 'dream home' – have a look at the strugglers on one of the TV home-buying shows. If you saved up £100k, your perfect house likely costs £120k. If you saved up £1 million, your perfect home will be £1.3 million (how annoying! Imagine the suffering...). It will hence help you to limit your options to those that are affordable and not spend weeks agonising about options out of reach. Here we look at factors that determine how much, roughly, you can afford to pay for your own digs.

2.2.1 What can the property cost?

When you come to think of how much you can spend on your own home, you can be super logical about your upper limit:

- Banks are likely to lend you around 4 times your annual pre-tax wage if you are alone or around 3 times the joint annual pre-tax wage if you buy together. You might get more depending on the lender and your personal circumstances. Practically, this might look like this:

  - Lone buyer: Annual pre-tax wage: £25,000

    Likely maximum mortgage: £100,000

  - Couple: Joint annual pre-tax wage: £50,000

    Likely maximum mortgage: £150,000

- Next you need to know the amount of your deposit. As a first time buyer, you will get away with a 5% deposit. If you have less than that, you are unlikely to get a mortgage, or you will get very unfavourable terms.

- Next you need to figure out what the whole process will cost you.

- To refine, you need to decide over what term you want to pay off the mortgage, and what your maximum monthly mortgage payments are.

- Sort out these figures, and you'll get the rough maximum price you can pay.

To make this thought process more transparent, here are several examples. These examples plan for a good chunk of money required for outstanding rent, moving, basic furniture as well as repairs in the new home. Always budget for repairs, and always have enough cash in the bank if your boiler packs up, bird smashes through the window or roof gets a hole.

In the examples below, the total cost for the property assumes a 5% deposit (calculate this as your deposit divided by 0.05). If you have more savings can put down a 10%, 15% or an even higher deposit, you will get much better mortgage interest rates! But we look at this a bit later.

Table 5. Example #1 –A first time buyer with £25,000 pre-tax income and matching deposit. Balanced match between savings and bank loan.

Item	£
Annual wage (pre-tax)	£25,000
The deposit you saved up	+ £10,000
Solicitor cost	- £1,200
Survey + Fees	- £1000
Moving, furniture and repairs	- £3,000
Your amount of cash for deposit after costs	+£4,800
What you could afford at a 5% deposit	£ 96,000
What the bank might lend you	£100,000
Cost of property	**£96,000**

Table 6. Example #2 – A first time buyer with £35,000 pre-tax income and small deposit. Constrained by deposit.

Item	£
Annual wage (pre-tax)	£35,000
The deposit you saved up	+ £5,000
Solicitor cost	- £1,200
Survey + Fees	- £1000
Moving, furniture and repairs	- £3,000
Your amount of cash for deposit after costs	- £200
Maximum cost of property at 5% deposit	Forget it
What the bank might lend you (with more savings)	£140,000
Cost of property (constrained by deposit)	**£0**

Table 7. Example #3 –A first time buyer with £35,000 pre-tax income and small deposit who cashes in on some perks. Still constrained by deposit.

Item	£
Annual wage (pre-tax)	£35,000
The deposit you saved up	+ £5,000
Help to Buy ISA bonus	+ £1,600
Mortgage cash back	+£500
Solicitor cost	- £1,200
Survey + Fees	- £1000
Moving, furniture and repairs (+£1000 cash back)	- £2,000
Your amount of cash for deposit after costs	+ £2,900
Maximum cost of property	£58,000
What the bank might lend you (with more savings)	£140,000
Cost of property (constrained by deposit)	**£58,000**

Table 8. Example #4 – A first time buyer with £35,000 pre-tax income and huge deposit. Constrained by salary.

Item	£
Annual wage (pre-tax)	£35,000
The deposit you saved up	+ £30,000
Solicitor cost	- £1,200
Survey + Fees	- £1000
Moving, furniture and repairs	- £3,000
Your amount of cash for deposit after costs	+ £24,800
Maximum cost of property at 5% deposit	£496,000
What the bank might lend you	£140,000
Cost of property* (constrained by salary)	**£147,368**
Your actual required deposit for that (5% deposit)	£7,368

Table 9. Example #5 – A couple with joint £70,000 pre-tax income and sizeable joint deposit.

Item	£
Joint annual wage (pre-tax)	£70,000
The deposit you saved up together	+ £30,000
Solicitor cost	- £1,200
Survey + Fees	- £1000
Moving, furniture and repairs	- £3,000
Your amount of cash for deposit after costs	+ £24,800
Maximum cost of property at 5% deposit	£496,000
What the bank might lend you (3x joint salary)	£210,000
Cost of property* (constrained by salary)	**£221,052**
Your actual required deposit for that (5% deposit)	£11,052

* You calculate this so that what the bank lends you is 95% of the purchase price since your deposit covers the remaining 5%. That brings the possible price up a little.

2.2.2 Credit score

What a bank will lend you will depend on your credit score. You can check your score for example here:

https://www.checkmyfile.com/

or here:

https://www.experian.co.uk/

Check out first whether this will leave a 'footprint' – every time you do a hard credit check, it will be on your file. Too many checks (e.g. when opening several bank accounts over a short time period) might lower your credit score.

As mentioned in Chapter 1. , one easy thing to do for a good credit score is to regularly spend money on your credit card and pay it back. This will develop your history of reliable repayments. It doesn't have to be much, just £100 or a few hundred each month. The main thing is that you can show that you repay your debt.

If you have outstanding debt, try to clear it before going for a mortgage and discuss with a financial advisor. The UK has a big debt problem, and you have to protect yourself from your finances getting out of hand.

2.3 Running costs

Before you can work out the monthly payments you can afford, have a look through the costs below and estimate the approximate running costs of your new home. Subtract this from your available funds that you can pay each month, and that is your maximum repayment.

When you think about how much you can pay each month, consider the following:

- Don't plan for everything you earn! You can always make overpayments on a mortgage, but you'll get into trouble if you can't keep up. Especially if you are on a tracker mortgage, your rate might go up swiftly, where suddenly you have to pay a lot more each month. Often, banks advise to budget for a 10% increase in interest rate.

- How would you bridge a gap if things get rough – can you build up savings or plan ahead with overpayments?

- Keep some money back for repairs.

- Don't think you'll be able to suddenly live for the next 10 years on a low budget. Old habits die hard. Look at how much you currently spend each month and on what. Prepare a first budget assuming that you will continue with your current lifestyle.

2.3.1 New monthly costs for homeowners

When you own your property, you will encounter new monthly costs that you did not have before. The whole chapter 'Running Costs' looks at these new costs in context of all your other monthly costs. So to start with, have a look at costs you may not have met before which you have to budget for. Before you despair, remember that you will save on all the rent you are currently paying. So it would be surprising if overall you would pay more in new costs than you would save in rent given that you are building up equity with your purchase. The tables below illustrate this.

Table 10. New monthly running costs that you may encounter when you go from rented to owning your own house. **Bold** are those costs that you will almost certainly have to pay. Depending on your rental arrangement, some of the other costs may be included in your contract and be unfamiliar to you, but most likely you are already paying them (such as internet bills and council tax).

Item	Monthly cost
Buildings insurance	**£20 to £30**
Contents insurance	£5 to £10
Life and critical illness insurance	**£25 to £50+**
Repayment: interest ('lost' money)	**£100 to £300+**
Repairs and servicing	**£20 to £500+**
Council Tax	£80 to £120+
Other insurances	£20 to £60+
Service Charge	£20 to £100+
Parking charge	£5 to £30+
Phone bills	£15 to £30+
Internet and TV	£20 to £40+

Table 11. Comparison between extra monthly costs and savings from not renting (here: £600) based on an example for a property costing around £200,000, being paid off over 15 years. For repayment, have a think about what you will 'lose' in paying interest. The remainder of what you pay off for the house is still yours in capital, it is just bound in the house. This is different from renting, where you would never be able to see the monthly rent that you are paying again when you move out, as you can't sell.

Item	Monthly cost
Buildings insurance	-£21
Contents insurance	-£6
Life and critical illness insurance	-£40
Repayment: interest portion ('lost' money)	-£150
Extra cost associated with owning	-£217
Saving in rent ('lost' money)	+£600
Balance*	+400

* This does not take into account costs of repairs and servicing, which you will have to cover.

In the following sections, we will have a closer look at a lot of the monthly running costs you will or may encounter, both the new ones and the ones you are already paying.

2.3.2 Insurance

Buildings insurance

This is likely a new cost. Buildings insurance has the purpose to cover the cost of rebuilding your home if it gets damaged or destroyed. Mortgage providers typically make it a requirement to take out this cover. Anyway, you would be a little daft not to, as it is the only way of managing the risk of e.g. a fire. Buildings Insurance normally covers the following:

- The structure of your home, roofs, walls, also including fences, gates and outbuildings. It should also include permanent fixtures like kitchens, bathrooms and fitted wardrobes.

- Weather events, such as storms, floods, earthquakes, lightning. This may be conditional on living outside flood risk zones.

- Fire, explosion and smoke.

- Theft, attempted theft and vandalism.

- Water or oil leaking from pipes or heating systems.

- Frozen and burst pipes.

- Fallen trees, branches, lampposts, aerials or satellite dishes.

- Subsidence (there will be exemptions).

- Vehicle or aircraft collisions.

You might also get

- Alternative accommodation.

- Emergency support.

- Legal expenses.

- ...and other options

The cost of insurance varies widely depending on the size of your home, the age, the area and any additional extras you may want. Budget £200 to £300 per year for an average home as a starting point, hence around £21 per month. Be aware of the excess you will have to pay and what is not covered; for example, a broken heating system drowning your home might result in the insurance paying for all works to repair damage to a fitted kitchen, but not the required plumbing to repair the cause of the leak.

Contents insurance

This is likely a new cost. As opposed to buildings insurance, contents insurance covers the stuff inside your home that is not fixed. Often, you can buy the two insurances together. Contents are covered for damage from events such as fire/floods/storms/natural disasters, vandalism or theft. Remember, a leaking heating system is not a flood. Accidental damage (spilling wine on a carpet) usually costs extra. For items you take outside your home, you also usually have to go for an add-on. Here are several choices you can typically make:

- Excess – how much do you pay towards each claim? This impacts the premium. You can play around with different options.

- Named items worth more than around £2,000 each.

- Contents you take outside (iPods, mobiles, cameras, laptops etc.).

- Accidental damage.

- Legal advice.

- Bicycle cover.

- Cash.

- ...and other options

Make sure you get a policy that replaces 'new for old'. Contents insurance is not compulsory, and you have to weigh up how much you would pay for it and how much all your stuff is worth. Budget around £75 per year as a starting point, hence around £6.25 per month.

Life and critical illness insurance

This is likely a new cost. It does what it says on the tin and will usually be offered to you at your mortgage appointment, or at least a quote. It might not be compulsory.

Critical illness insurance will take care of your mortgage if you become ill with cancer or something similar. Typically, it pays off your mortgage in full should this happen to you, so you can focus on not dying. This sounds dark, but it will give you peace of mind that you won't lose your house in a moment where the odds are against you.

Life insurance will pay your partner or dependents a lump sum in the event of your death, which should usually pay off the mortgage. This means that if something happens to you, those who are left behind don't suddenly lose their home.

To get this type of insurance, you usually need to complete a medical questionnaire, and costs will depend on a lot of factors. Most importantly, it will depend on the cost of your purchase, as that is what the insurance would buy out. Budget around £30 to £40 per month as a starting point for an average property.

Mortgage Payment Protection Insurance

These days, if you lose your job, the government won't help you with your mortgage payments at all for nine months, and after that will likely only cover interest. This may be less of a problem if you buy jointly or have rich parents, but if you are on your own, losing your job is a risk that might lose you your home. If your contract and/or employer have supportive sick pay and redundancy payout policies, you also less at risk than if working for an employer who will leave you with (hardly) nothing.

Mortgage Payment Protection Insurance (MPPI) jumps in if you fall on hard times, such as due to sickness, an accident or loss of your job (redundancy, employer default etc.). This insurance pays for your mortgage payments (up to a certain amount capped by your income and/or the mortgage amount) and some even pay for costs such as council tax by awarding 125% of the mortgage repayment.

Other potential insurances

You can shop around for further insurances to suit your lifestyle, however we won't go into detail for them as there are too many options.

Will

Fair enough, this is not quite an insurance, but you might also want to budget for a will. This is important if your partner is not the joint owner for example. Check with a solicitor how much this would cost and what you should do.

2.3.3 Council tax

Everyone has to pay council tax, unless you are a student or receive certain benefits. You will most likely be familiar with this from renting. Council tax will depend on the size of your home and the rates of the council covering the area where you are buying. You can look this up in advance, for example here:

https://www.gov.uk/council-tax

Council tax varies widely, but budget around £1,200 per year for an average home in a city, hence around £100 per month.

2.3.4 Bills

Bills for owning a home are actually pretty much the same compared to what you already know from renting. Below are the top three.

Gas

You typically need gas for the heating and hot water system as well as for some hobs. You can shop around amongst providers to get the best deal, and remember to check your tariff every half a year or so to make sure you are not being ripped off. Be aware that costs for gas fluctuate wildly between winter and summer, as you usually only need the central heating in the colder months. If you are on a normal monthly tariff, this should account for that, so that your monthly payments cover the total cost across the year. You can budget around £50 to £60 per month for a 3-bedroom house as a starting point.

Electricity

Yep, it keeps the lights on and things powered. If you have electric heating, it will weigh in heavily. You can budget around £30 to £60 per month for a 3-bedroom house as a starting point.

Water

Water also includes sewage/waste water. While you might still be renting in a house that is not on a meter, purchasing a home often makes installation of a meter compulsory. Check for your council. You can budget around £35 per month for a 2-person household as a starting point.

2.3.5 Charges

Service charge (flats and some new builds)

Watch out for this one! Flats and many new builds come with a service charge, which includes landscaping and maintaining the estate. This can be anything from £50 per year to £100+ per month. Find out about this before committing to any property, as you can't get rid of it. To make matters worse, you can't even really do anything if charges go up while you live there. These charges are best avoided through choice of property, but that can be easier said than done.

Parking charge

Not super common, but this could add some more to your monthly bills. Find out before committing.

2.3.6 Regular outgoings/living costs

It will help you to have a closer look at your current finances when planning for the road ahead. Here is a list of the most common regular outgoings you should account for:

- Student loan
- Phone bills
- Internet and TV
- Car maintenance and petrol
- Public transport
- Food
- Clothes
- Medications
- Private pension
- Health and dental insurance
- Travel insurance
- Holidays
- Pets
- Smoking and other addictions
- Hobbies
- Pocket money

Draw up a list of all these regular costs below and add items that are important for you. As mentioned above – old habits die hard. Budget for your current lifestyle, and take it from there.

2.3.7 Putting it all together

After having a look at all the running costs involved, let's put it all together. The below examples illustrate what running costs can sum up to, but should only be regarded as guidelines. The bottom line is: running your own home and life costs around £1,000 per month, so this still has to be part of the thinking once you think about your mortgage repayments next. As the table illustrates, if you have pets, are addicted to smoking and have a lot of hobbies while paying into a private pension, you might easily hit a monthly running cost of £2,000. That's one person's wage gone.

Table 12. Approximate monthly running costs for a 3-bedroom house. **Bold** are those items that are new when you own a home. *: most common items. Not included are your monthly mortgage repayments, which we will look at in Section 2.4.

Item	Approximate monthly cost
Buildings insurance*	**£21**
Contents insurance	£6
Life and critical illness insurance*	**£40**
Repairs and servicing*	**£50**
Council tax*	£100
Gas*	£50
Electricity*	£50
Water*	£35
Service Charge	**£50**
Parking charge	**£15**
Student loan	£75
Phone bills*	£20
Internet and TV*	£30
Car maintenance and petrol	£75
Public transport	£50

Item	Approximate monthly cost
Food*	£300
Clothes*	£100
Medications	£50
Private pension	£300
Health and dental insurance	£75
Travel insurance	£6
Holidays*	£50
Pets	£100
Smoking and other addictions	£250
Hobbies*	£100
Pocket money*	£200
Total: everything	£2,198
Total: most common items (* items)	**£1,221**

2.3.8 A first glance at your own scenario

Considering the potential costs listed in this chapter, you can draw up your own list of costs. Tables for this are included in the appendix, and for your convenience, here are some for a first go:

Your monthly living costs

Item	Monthly cost
Student loan	
Phone bills	
Internet and TV	
Car maintenance and petrol	
Public transport	
Food	

Item	Monthly cost
Clothes	
Medications	
Private pension	
Health- and/or dental insurance	
Travel insurance	
Holidays	
Pets	
Smoking and other addictions	
Hobbies	
Pocket money	
Other:	
Other:	
Other:	
Other:	
Total	

Your monthly running costs

Item	Monthly cost
Buildings insurance	
Contents insurance	
Life and critical illness insurance	
Council tax	
Gas	
Electricity	
Water	
Service Charge	
Parking charge	

Item	Monthly cost
Other:	
Other:	
Other:	
Other:	
Total	

Your expected total monthly costs

Item	Monthly cost
Total living costs	
Total running costs	
Other:	
Total	

2.3.9 More info

- Information about council tax can be found here:

  https://www.gov.uk/council-tax

- Advice on insurances from the Citizen's Advice Bureau can be found here:

  https://www.citizensadvice.org.uk/consumer/insurance/insurance/types-of-insurance/

- Tips and advice on costs that will hit a homeowner can be found here:

  https://www.which.co.uk/money/mortgages-and-property/first-time-buyers/the-household-bills-youll-pay-as-a-homeowner-akcpd2b821cn

2.3.10 Who can help

A good first point of call is actually the free mortgage advice offered by many estate agents. They will run through your budget and give you a first idea what you can afford. They will try to sell you their services through this initial pitch. And yes, it is normally free!

2.4 What monthly repayments can I afford?

Now that you know how much your new home can cost roughly and what your approximate monthly costs are, the next step is to work out how much you can repay each month for any mortgage you have to take out on it. This is important to know when you walk into a mortgage appointment and when you plan your future ahead.

2.4.1 Mortgage constraints

After working out all the figures for the cost of your property and monthly running costs, now you can start thinking about what mortgage repayments you can realistically cover every month. We will go into more detail of mortgages in the next chapter, but there are a few important considerations:

- Is your mortgage rate fixed for the whole term of part of the term?

- Are you on a tracker mortgage that may go up if the UK interest base rate goes up?

- How safe is your job and income and what is your outlook?

- How much flexibility do you need for unforeseen expenditures?

- Are you planning on having kids?

- Who can save you if something goes wrong?

Questions like the ones above should help you decide how much of your monthly household income you want to put into your mortgage. Remember, this is the amount that the bank will come chasing. You can always pay more than your agreed repayment – typically 10% of the initial mortgage amount per year on a fixed mortgage (you can pay more, but you have to pay fees), and an unlimited amount on a tracker.

To plan for these eventualities, you can do the following calculations:

- Monthly savings to let you bridge any unforeseen gaps.

- What would the mortgage be like if the interest rate increased by 10%? Make sure you could still cover that.

Your mortgage lender will give you an indication of the maximum monthly repayments that they 'trust' you with. The purpose of this is to protect yourself from running out of money. Similar to the whole mortgage amount, this is usually based on your annual income, but in addition also on your monthly outgoings.

2.4.2 Monthly repayments: affordability

To figure out how much you can repay every month, make a simple table that contains:

- Your (joint) monthly take-home pay

- Your anticipated running and living costs estimated in the chapter above

- Any savings you wish to be able to make (important in order to cover unforeseen repairs or illness)

Sprinkle this with an assumed 10% increase in mortgage rates to leave a bit of a buffer.

Once you know your maximum monthly mortgage payment, the cost of your property and your deposit, the mortgage duration will fall out of this equation.

Table 13. Example #1 – Monthly repayments. A couple buying a 3-bedroom house and considering associated costs. Depending on the flexibility this couple would like to have, they could think about committing £900 to £1,800 each month for the mortgage.

Item	Amount
Joint annual wage (pre-tax)	£70,000
Joint annual take-home pay	£54,366
Joint monthly take-home pay	£4,531
Running and living costs	£1,500

Item	Amount
Planned savings	£1,000
Leftover	£2,031
Assumed 10% increase in monthly mortgage repayment for all your leftovers	£200
What you could commit to if you go all out	**£1,831**
10% overpayment allowance on e.g. £160,000 mortgage	£1,333
Knowing you can always pay MORE, lower commitment*	**£900**
Planned overpayment within 10% margin	£900

*This is very subjective – the lower your commitment, the longer the mortgage term. Once you get playing around with mortgage calculators, you can fine-tune this balance. Your bank advisor should also be able to help make the final decision.

In the Appendix you can plug these numbers together for your own circumstances, and here is a copy of that table:

Your monthly repayment scenario

Item	Amount
Joint annual wage (pre-tax)	
Joint annual take-home pay	
Joint monthly take-home pay	
Running and living costs (from previous table)	
Planned savings	
Leftover	
Assumed 10% increase in mortgage cost	
What you could commit to if you go all out	
10% overpayment	
Knowing you can always pay MORE, lower commitment*	
Planned overpayment within 10% margin	

2.4.3 More info

- A basic income tax calculator can be found here where you can look at your gross and net pay:

  https://www.moneysavingexpert.com/tax-calculator/

- Good general advice on mortgages can be found here:

  https://www.moneysavingexpert.com/mortgages/

2.4.4 Who can help

All major banks should be able to get you in front of a mortgage advisor, with whom you can go through your personal scenario and work out the best mortgage option for your circumstances. This is free and typically results in a mortgage offer in principle. Just make sure you book in advance and allow around 2 hours for the appointment.

2.5 Is it worth it?

If you look at expert advice, the answer is pretty much always: Yes. Unless you buy in an area where house prices are going down, your mortgage will be similar to your rent, but you track the market and build up capital. If you want to move, you sell it on.

The only thing to remember here is that each time you sell and buy again, it will cost you around £5,000 to £10,000 in agent fees, solicitor fees, moving fees, potential stamp duty and other things that need to be done. So if you are planning on moving around a lot and prefer a flexible lifestyle, buying might cost you more than renting and it will do your head in with all the administrative hassle. But remember, you can also always have a lodger and you can make arrangements to rent out your home – there will just be some changes in the mortgage arrangement and you will pay tax on rent if the tenant is not your lodger.

Whole books have been written about why buying is worth it, if you want to read more opinions on buying in detail. While the conclusion is typically to buy, these books have not yet caught up with the effect Brexit may have. There has been a slow-down in the property market leading up to this sorry event. Depending on the final outcome of negotiations, there is a risk of a house market crash. At the same time, should there be a favourable outcome, the market which is currently slow may pick up really quickly again, making prices more expensive. No-one can tell at the moment.

2.5.1 More info

The Home Owners Alliance has a neat and compact decision help if you are not sure whether you should buy:

https://hoa.org.uk/advice/guides-for-homeowners/i-am-buying/is-buying-right-for-me-2/

Chapter 3

Basic ingredients

3. BASIC INGREDIENTS

This chapter looks at what we call the 'basic ingredients' for buying your own home. When you embark on the journey, you will have to work closely with several stakeholders that you may have never interacted with before. You may feel completely out of your depth and as a consequence just run with the easiest option that may not be the best one. In this chapter, we hence look at the following lot in detail to prepare you for what is to come once you get going on your house hunt:

- Agents: what they do and what services they offer.

- Solicitors: what they (are supposed to) do, how to find one, what the costs may be and how to not lose your mind over them.

- Surveyors: what they do, how to find one and the general types of survey you can get.

- Mortgages: Basics about mortgages, the differences between fixed and tracker rates, interest rates, terms, loan-to-value (LTV) and useful practical tips.

- The property: types of ownership, different types of houses and other properties (flats, new builds, build-your-own).

3.1 Agents

3.1.1 What do agents do

The role of the property agent is to:

- Act on behalf of the vendor to advise on the sale and show you round properties.

- Give you information on the property which you request during or after viewing.

- Manage the negotiation between you and the vendor.

- Liaise during the conveyancing process and help pushing the sale through (well, sometimes).

First off: remember, the agent is paid by the vendor and will do everything in their power to get the vendor a good deal. Also, in most cases agents are paid a commission on a sale, so the more they shift the property for, the more they get. Profit maximisation is therefore definitely a big part of the agent's thinking. At the same time, agents will scan you whether you will make a good buyer; look at the chapter of getting prepared and drafting a bid pitch. An agent will also be concerned with making a good and functional sale happen, since they will only get their bonus once the property changed hands. If there is not a lot of interest in a house, the agent may talk sense into the seller to sell the property at the price you can afford, rather than waiting around for months for some loony who would pay a lot more.

Make sure you are friendly with the agent – they are only humans, too. If the agent likes you and has a good impression of you, you have better chances of getting their support, especially if there are lots of buyers.

Agents may have too many properties on their books to remember details about each of them. Also, the person showing you round may not be the sales negotiator and might be unfamiliar with the property. Give them time to find out details and get back to you. Always feel free to ask questions about the buying process and what to look for in a home. Some agents are very friendly and help you during your first steps figuring out what to look for.

Make sure you get everything important from the agent in writing. You will find that at the point of viewing and offering, you are promised the world. Once you get to the end of the conveyancing process, a lot of this can be forgotten about. Agents know what will make you bite. If they got you on the hook, at least have their lure in writing.

3.1.2 Getting on property alert lists

If you speak to an estate agent, you can get on the firm's property alert list based on your preferences. This could mean that you get informed about new properties coming onto the market before they are listed on e.g. Rightmove. Although this is not super common, it doesn't hurt to sign up. Many agents sign you up compulsory when you call to view a property. The downside is that the agent will know your budget – if they know you have £200,000 but are bidding for a home listed at £175,000, it will be harder to haggle them down.

3.1.3 Services affiliated with the agent

Broker and support

Once you start making contact with agents, pretty much every single one will offer you a free mortgage appointment, which may come under various names. Some agents even make this conditional of signing up with them. During these appointments, you will work out the rough mortgage you could get (which you may already have worked out yourself), you will get initial financial advice and you will hear a variety of promises in exchange for using their services. This may range from preferential early bird viewings to £1,000 off the purchase price if signing up. You will be invited to be supported through the sales process by an 'independent' broker, often working from the agent's back office. For £500 to £1,500, you would gain a personal broker to sort out a mortgage and push through your purchase. Whether or not you want this is your choice. You can certainly compare their mortgage rates to those of banks you are considering. If the person is good, he/she might help you manage the stress along the way. If not, it will just be another person to chase, and a lot of money in the bin.

Solicitor

When your offer on a house is accepted, agents will offer to link you up with a solicitor. The promise is typically that this will allow the agent to frequently chase your solicitor on your behalf and make sure the purchase goes through quicker and smoother than usual. It is unclear what the evidence is for this and most likely depends on the individual estate agent and the solicitors they work with. Fact is that it will add around £500 to your solicitor bill compared to the fees quoted independently. The agent may also use the local solicitor you were considering anyway, or a random solicitor halfway across the country. This is out of your control – you cannot vet or choose your assigned solicitor.

3.1.4 Who can help

- If you run into problems with an estate agent, the first line of attack is to resolve issues with him/her directly and, failing that, with the head of the firm or head of the office.

- If the agent is member of the National Association of Estate Agents (NAEA), you can seek advice and bring forward a complaint via them:

  http://www.naea.co.uk/

- If your agent belongs to the Ombudsman for Estate Agents (OEA) / Property Ombudsman (TPO), you can seek advice and bring forward a complaint via them. The OEA has more power than the NAEA.

  https://www.tpos.co.uk/

- If neither of the above can help, you can speak to the Citizen's Advice Bureau (CAB) or trading standards.

3.2 Solicitors

3.2.1 Solicitor vs. conveyancer

For ease of reading, we will refer to solicitors and conveyancers jointly as 'solicitors' in this book. It is important to note that all solicitors can be conveyancers, but not all conveyancers are solicitors. Becoming a solicitor requires more education than becoming a conveyancer, and you can expect a solicitor to have much broader legal background knowledge. At the same time, solicitors may deal with all sorts of other things: divorce, criminal law or other matters. Conveyancers only deal with property purchases day in, day out. Whether or not this matters for your purchase is not always clear. Just be aware of the different training backgrounds people may come from. Because solicitors are broader trained, they often cost a bit more than conveyancers. The conveyancing process, whether conducted by a solicitor or conveyancers, should however be near identical. Both, solicitors and conveyancers, should be certified and regulated – working with one that cannot demonstrate this may be a risky endeavour.

3.2.2 What do solicitors do?

The solicitor will be the legal arm of the purchase, handling all legal matters, acting as a buffer for moving money between stakeholders and running the due diligence (background check) on the property. The solicitor is basically the person in charge of legally transferring home ownership, a process which typically includes:

- Managing the sale after you had an offer accepted.

- Setting up your contract.

- Running 'searches' (see Chapter 8. Section 8.3.2 for more details).

- Raising enquiries with the vendor's solicitor.

- Potentially putting forward a re-negotiation.

- Handling deposit and mortgage payments.

- Register your title deeds.

- Handle your payment of stamp duty.

- Hand over the keys (unless done by the agent or otherwise).

3.2.3 Finding one

Pretty much everyone who ever bought a house will have horror stories to tell about their solicitor and the conveyancing process. Brace yourself that you might be no exception. The best way to find a great solicitor (the 1 in 100) is to pick a specific person who has been personally recommended by someone you trust and who has worked with that solicitor before. Else all bets are off. If you go from low to low, remember you are not alone – most other homebuyers have gone through the same experience before you, somehow made it through and now own their place. You'll forget the pain once you made it. With this pessimistic prelude, let's have a look at the basics of solicitors and attempts at controlling the damage.

What makes a 'good' solicitor?

So, finding a good solicitor is hard. Ideally, this is what you want from your solicitor:

- Being proactive and getting the best outcome for you.

- Chase the vendor's solicitor twice a week to keep the case moving.

- Read through all information they are supplied and detect errors, misrepresentation, discrepancies and issues requiring attention.

- Be diligent and precise, not making mistakes.

- Be familiar with your case.

- Answer open questions.

- Keep you in the loop.

- Be reachable by phone email and respond to you, ideally same day or next day.

If you are unlucky, your solicitor won't do any of that.

How do you find a solicitor?

In absence of any recommendation, you can look for firms or individuals online. You can also ask other people whom you get to know during the process, for example a good surveyor.

You can find licensed conveyancers on the CLC (Council of Licensed Conveyancers) website here, which should be unbiased:

https://www.clc-uk.org.uk/cms/cms.jsp?menu_id=19871

You can find solicitors through the Law Society's database here, which again should be unbiased:

http://solicitors.lawsociety.org.uk/

Then there are a range of web services that offer quotes. For example, you can use the services below to get a first idea how much conveyancing might cost you; this may be biased, as firms listed may pay a referral fee:

https://www.reallymoving.com

https://www.moneysupermarket.com/conveyancing/

https://hoa.org.uk/services/homeowners-alliance-conveyancing/

If you find interesting offers, do your due diligence: dismantle the offer to see whether there hidden fees, have a look how good ratings are, see what the exception clauses are. Have a look at the next section and compile a table of quotes.

When you know which individual would carry out the work, check the following:

- Can they meet your expected exchange and completion timeline?

- Do they NOT have a holiday booked before completion?

- Do they offer the communication mode you prefer?

Take a few days to think about options and have a look at people's ratings on trustworthy sources.

Looking at the details of the offering

Most solicitors will offer promises such as 8-12 week to completion or on-the-day response times. These adverts can be entirely made up, since no-one checks and if it does not happen for you, you'll be told you are just an unusual case. Sadly, you don't have much power in the face of a lawyer. Hence, be careful basing you choice on adverts and 'stats'. Also be careful basing your choice on someone's self-written profile; it might be to the contrary of that person's actual behaviour and performance.

When you look at offers, you can check the following points:

- Are all costs included in the quote or could there be hidden fees? Make sure you are told ALL fees for your scenario and that you are given a list of all potential additional items/services and their associated fees. Check whether quotes are inclusive or exclusive of VAT.

- What will you pay if you don't complete? Some firms don't charge certain fees if you don't complete or your purchase falls through.

- How does the quote and service compare to other firms in the area and nationally?

- Is there any independent rating available? What does it say?

You can then start to draw up a comparison table for yourself, with costs roughly funnelled into the categories in Section 3.2.4. You can then make an informed choice of whom you want to proceed with. Remember, once you picked your solicitor and started the conveyancing process, it will be hard to change your mind.

Location

Remember your solicitor doesn't have to be local – if you know a good one at the other end of the country, you are free to work with that person. It shouldn't make a difference, except for the potential need to travel there to do things in person.

Size of the firm and holiday/sickness cover

If you use a bigger firm, your solicitor should be covered for when they go on holiday. This might sound minor, but you may find that you lose a month in the run-up to (and fall-out of) a solicitors 2-3 week summer holiday during conveyancing high season. If the firm has several staff and you kick up a fuss, at least there is a chance your sale will not stall.

Using the estate agent's recommendation

As mentioned in the previous sections, most – if not all – estate agents will offer you a solicitor service once you agreed on a sale. The main reasons to run with this is typically given as the agent being able to directly push the solicitor and move your purchase forward quicker. This may or may not be the case; it really depends how good the working relationship between agent and solicitor is, and this varies on a case-by-case basis. However, there are also tangible downsides to this arrangement:

- It will cost you more. The agent will receive a commission from the solicitor, which in turn is passed on to you. Expect to pay around £500 more.

- You usually have no control over the choice of firm and person who will do your conveyancing, so you are at the mercy of whomever the agent has on their books and who is available.

- Flogging the solicitor is often a required standard upsale resulting in extra bonus for the agent. However, there should not be hard feelings if you say no – they will offer it to anyone.

If you don't want to use the agent's solicitor, you can also do a light-touch approach. You can ask which firms the estate agent would recommend, as those are often at least of reasonable quality. Estate agents should also be able to give you feedback if you have shortlisted solicitors, as they might have had bad experiences with some. If a solicitor does not show up for completion, the agent's sale is in trouble – they won't recommend that one! Once the agent knows that you are not using their service, they'll be happy to advise you since their commission depends on the successful and timely sale, too.

Online options

There seem to be more and more online solicitors now. Be careful about this, as you cannot go and knock on someone's door if they screw up. However, if you are fine with a less personal approach, an online conveyance/solicitor might suit you. As for all other options, do your due diligence:

- Check their reviews through trustworthy / independent websites

- Check they are regulated and certified

- Check whether you will have contact with one individual or rather a call centre

- Check what the modes of contact are

If you find quotes that are too good to be true, they probably are. Have a think whether saving a few hundred Pounds is worth the risk of later having to sue your solicitor because they made a mistake. It is most likely not worth the stress.

3.2.4 How much does it cost?

The conveyancing process costs a lot, and costs are a combination of fees for work, fees for simple administrative items and costs such as searches. The typical fees paid to a solicitor are given as an example below. Beware that there may be additional fees such as release of the Help to Buy ISA for £60 and a range of additional offerings, such an extended area search including school ratings for around £75. Your solicitor will provide a list with additional chargeable items, which might exceed one A4 page. Make sure you check this and get a broken-down quote in writing before signing up for anything.

Table 14. Approximate fees associated with the solicitor for the whole conveyancing process (guideline figures only).

Activity	Approx. cost
Legal fees	£600*
Bank transfer charge	£40
SDLT return	£85

Activity	Approx. cost
Checks and documentation	£55
Land registry fee	£100
Searches (basic: local, water/drainage etc)	£320
Total	**£1200**

This could vary between £550 and £800 or more. Check whether it's incl. or excl. VAT as well.

3.2.5 How to not lose your nerves

This is a tough one. As basic anger management and rehabilitation exercises, we recommend the following:

- Breathe. Count from 10 backwards. Breathe deeper.

- Keep a written timeline of your solicitor's actions and failings. You can use this for a future complaint and to stop your mind mulling over things again and again.

- Keep a written timeline of progress. Tick off things that have been done. Every little step will feel great. A log is included in the appendix of this book.

- Watch something funny.

- Talk to a friend who is going through the same horror.

For tips on managing your solicitor, please look at the detailed process and tips in Chapter 8.

3.2.6 More info

- The Solicitor Regulation Authority (SRA) offers online help and guidance for the process of engaging and working with a solicitor:

  https://www.sra.org.uk/consumers/find-use-instruct-solicitor.page

- The Council for Licensed Conveyancers offers online help and guidance for engaging and working with a conveyancer:

  https://www.clc-uk.org/

- The Home Owners Alliance (HOA) offers a very good overview over the conveyancing process:

  https://hoa.org.uk/advice/guides-for-homeowners/i-am-buying/#section_7

3.2.7 Who can help

- The Solicitors Regulation Authority can help with problems relating to misconduct etc:

  https://www.sra.org.uk/home/home.page.

  You can also call them about general enquiries and they will point you in the right direction. The turnaround time for a complaint is around 10 days.

- The Financial Ombudsman deals with service-related issues:

  http://www.financial-ombudsman.org.uk/.

  The turnaround time is around 8 weeks.

3.3 Surveyors

3.3.1 What do surveyors do?

Sadly, when buying a property, "Caveat Emptor" is the guiding principle: "Let the buyer beware". The home owner is not obliged to tell you anything, and it is your job to find out all the things that are wrong with the property. Hence, you need a kick-ass surveyor to help you spot issues that were painted over, DIY fixed and/or on the brink of collapse.

A surveyor will assess the state of the property you are buying. This means that someone with expertise will assess what repairs are needed, what further checks should be conducted, which aspects of the property may need building regulations approval etc. The surveyor will spend a few hours to a day at the property and look at everything. One of the exemptions is typically that they won't move furniture or trash – if the vendor placed a giant couch in front of a hole in the wall, they won't be able to report on it. The outcome of the survey visit is a survey report, ideally accompanied with images.

Remember that the surveyor will be on your side – you are paying him/her. However, at the same time, know that surveyors have to raise absolutely everything in the survey to make sure they are not later held accountable for overlooking a potential issue. This means that you should reality check recommended repairs and determine which ones are critical, urgent, beneficial or cosmetic. Usually, your surveyor will give you that information over the telephone. You can then plan and budget accordingly. For a fee, your surveyor may provide cost estimates for works highlighted in the survey.

The above holds true for a properly educated and experienced surveyor. If you wind up with a bimbo who has only learnt to drop text blocks into a home buyers report, you might not get many valuable insights beyond the obvious. So make sure to background-check your surveyor properly, especially if you are commissioning a substantial report.

3.3.2 Finding a good surveyor

When you look for a surveyor, going by recommendations can again be very helpful. Either way, make sure that your surveyor is a chartered surveyor and RICS registered:

https://www.rics.org/uk/.

Have a look at the training and history of you surveyor. Is it an estate agent who retrained or an individual with 30 years' experience in building pathology? Request a sample report to assess the quality and depth of the report. As with all good things, quality usually costs a little more. Since you are already blowing huge amounts of money on the process, paying a little more doesn't really matter but could provide you with high quality insights if you choose wisely.

When you select a surveyor, have a look at the following:

- Content of report. Get a list what the surveyor does as extra and standard.

- Who writes the report. Nowadays, survey reports can be written semi-automatically using pre-written text blocks. Check whether your surveyor writes the survey by hand or using text blocks.

- Location. In the case of a surveyor, locality might be a big bonus: your surveyor might already be familiar with issues specific to certain areas in your area. Also, you would not expect a surveyor to travel halfway across the country.

- Costs. Have a look at the cost for the different report types in context of what is on offer. Cheapest is not best, find a reasonable balance.

- Get-out clauses. See if the surveyor de-risks the process for you by offering get-out clauses, such as a partial refund after verbal feedback without a report if the property is a wreck, last-minute appointment rescheduling and other helpful mechanisms. This means that in a worst case scenario you could re-schedule the survey for a different home or hold it off if something comes up between the time of booking and survey date.

- Reviews. As with all services, have a look whether there are unbiased online reviews, for example on Google, Yell or Trustpilot.

- Turnaround times. Ask how long wait times are until you can get booked it, and how long you have to wait for the report after the survey was conducted.

- Communication. You will get a feel for how open your surveyor is to communication when making initial enquiries. You may need to follow-up on a survey with further enquiries, and it will be beneficial to work with someone who is prepared to keep communication channels open.

- Get the name of the individual who will actually carry out your survey. Check that they individual who will conduct your survey is actually a chartered RICS surveyor here:

  http://www.rics.org/uk/find-a-member/

  Be aware that only surveyors who are registered as MRICS or FRICS are fully qualified Chartered Surveyors. Make sure the person is a **Chartered Building Surveyor** – there are other types of chartered surveyor, which however do not have a targeted training background. Surveyors holding the AssocRICS are NOT chartered surveyors and trained to a lesser standard.

3.3.3 Types of survey

Generally, there are two types of survey: a HomeBuyers Report and a Building Survey. They will assess your property in different depth, and you need to decide which survey you find most appropriate for your property. Ask your surveyor which type of survey may be the most suitable for your circumstances.

HomeBuyer Report

This is a more 'superficial' report, providing a condition rating (on a scale from 1 to 3) for visible areas and permanent structures of the property in a systematic way.

The default RICS template includes the following sections:

- About the inspection
- Overall opinion and summary of the condition ratings
- About the property
- Outside the property
- Inside the property
- Services
- Grounds (including shared areas for flats)
- Issues for your legal advisers
- Risks
- Valuation

You can have a look at a template for example here:

https://www.homebuyeronline.co.uk/userFiles/file/Homebuyer%20Report%20Sample.pdf

The HomeBuyer Report is typically recommended for newer properties and those that are in good state of repair without significant alterations since they had been built.

Building Survey

The Building Survey is also called a 'Full Structural Survey' and is the more comprehensive and in-depth survey option. It will comment on structural aspects of the property inside and outside including roof space, test of services (shower, hob...), damp measurements, assessment for dry rot and wood worm.

Building surveys do usually not come in a default template like the HomeBuyer Report. Rather, their layout is specific to the individual surveyor. Great examples for excellent Building Surveys are here:

https://www.mpsurveys.co.uk/building-surveys

This type of survey is typically recommended for properties older than 50 years and those that had alterations undertaken, such as removal of internal walls or addition of extensions.

Other supplementary surveys

Aside from the above two standard surveys, you may decide to undertake further surveys. These may include assessment of

- Asbestos contamination

- Sulphate attack

- Subsistence

- Heave

... And other issues. These more specific assessments are typically brought up in the initial Building Survey, and potentially in the HomeBuyer report.

3.3.4 More info

The Royal Institute for Chartered Surveyors (RICS) offers online help and guidance on the survey process and finding a registered surveyor:

https://www.rics.org/uk/

3.3.5 Who can help

As above. Be wary of surveyors who work closely with the estate agent, as there may be a conflict of interest.

3.4 Mortgages

3.4.1 Basics

Most people need a mortgage to afford a home. There are different types of mortgage you can choose from, which are described in this section. The important thing with a mortgage is that you will only get one if you can put down a deposit. For first time buyers, this can be as little as 5%. But if you have not saved up enough to afford the costs described in the previous chapters plus the deposit all in one go, you will have to save up until you can.

When you choose a mortgage, you typically have the following questions to answer in order to establish which type of mortgage suits you best:

- Would you like to know exactly what your mortgage payment will be throughout the mortgage term?

- Can you afford to deal with variation in the mortgage rate, but need flexibility on paying the mortgage off faster (as in more than 10% of the initial mortgage value per year)?

- Do you need the ability to get out of the mortgage over the coming couple of years without re-mortgaging? For example, your job might take you abroad and you might sell up?

- Are you planning on settling down and would like to lock down a low interest rate for as long as possible?

Have a think about these questions. You should also get asked a lot of these questions at your mortgage appointment. Details about the corresponding mortgage options are in the sections below.

3.4.2 Fixed rate or tracker mortgage

There are two basic mortgage types: fixed rate and tracker mortgages.

Fixed rate mortgage

A fixed rate mortgage gives you the same interest rate throughout the time over which the interest is fixed. This is not to be confused with the mortgage term, which is usually longer than the period of the fixed rate. For example, you can take out a 20-year mortgage with a 5-year fixed interest rate at 2.6%. During the first five years, you will hence pay exactly that – 2.6% interest. After five years, you will have to pick a follow-on product. Should the interest rate have gone up to 5% then, that's tough luck.

Typically, you can choose to fix the selected interest rate for 1, 2, 3, 5 or 10 years. The longer the period, the higher the interest rate and the more complex will be the conditions attached to it. The most important factor to consider here is the **early repayment charge**: the table below compares example penalties for paying off your mortgage early.

Table 15. Illustrative early repayment charges for a 3-, 5- or 10-year fixed interest rate period. The penalty is typically paid on the remaining outstanding mortgage, although you are normally allowed to make a 10% overpayment.

Year	3-year period	5-year period	10-year period
1	3%	5%	8%
2	2%	4%	7%
3	1%	3%	7%
4	-	2%	7%
5	-	1%	6%
6	-	-	5%
7	-	-	4%
8	-	-	3%
9	-	-	2%
10	-	-	1%

The longer the interest rate period, the more you will have to fork up if you want to pay off early. So if you are on a rate with a 10-year period and after 1 year you win the lottery, you may have to pay 8% of the remaining mortgage value in penalties. Not that it would matter when winning the lottery. However, if you were to get a huge bonus, that penalty might actually prevent you from paying the mortgage off. If you change jobs and want to move abroad, it will also hurt. Remember this penalty – well, charge – usually doesn't apply if you move house and take the mortgage across.

The **upside** of a fixed rate mortgage includes:

- You exactly know how much you will pay each month for the duration of the fixed rate.

- If during the fixed-rate period the Bank of England base interest rate goes up, you won't suffer form it – you continue to pay what you signed up for.

The **downside** of a fixed rate mortgage includes:

- It typically limits how much you can overpay (pay extra on top of your regular mortgage payment in order to pay off the mortgage faster). This is typically 10% of the initial mortgage value. If you want to pay off more than 10% extra, you will incur a fine – or fee, depending on which side of the table you sit on.

- If during the fixed-rate period the interest rate drops, you won't benefit from it – you continue to pay what you signed up for.

The figure below illustrates the basic difference between fixed rate and tracker mortgage.

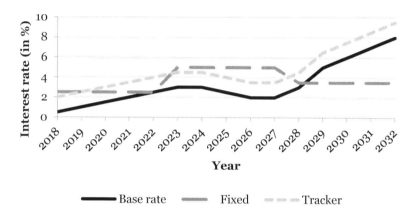

Figure 3. Illustration of Bank of England base rate, fixed rate mortgage and tracker mortgage. The **fixed rate** mortgage makes you pay a fixed amount of interest over an agreed period – here 5 years. This interest is defined at the start of that period. The **tracker mortgage** tracks the base rate by a certain percentage – here 1.5% throughout. You can see that depending on what the base rate does, the fixed rate or tracker mortgage may result in lower interest. If during the fixed rate period the base rate goes up, you might pay more on a tracker mortgage. If during the fixed rate period the base rate goes down, you might pay more on the fixed rate mortgage. Remember the tracker mortgage will also run over a defined period, although you can 'fix out' when you get cold feet.

Tracker mortgage

A tracker mortgage tracks the Bank of England base rate with a fixed extra percentage. For example, you might get a 1.8% tracker mortgage, which tracks the Bank of England base rate of 0.5% at 1.3%. The 0.5% can change any time, and your interest will change with it. The 1.3% is the fixed percentage sitting on top of this base rate which you sign up to. If something crazy happens in the Economy, the base rate can change very fast: this happened during the economic crash in 2008, when it dropped from more than 5% to 1% in just a year. Since March 2009, it has been fairly stable, bumbling along at 0.25% to 0.5%, recently (August 2018) going up to 0.75%. However, no-one knows what will happen to the base rate in 2, 5 or 10 years time from now. It is hard to imagine that it will drop below 0%. However, it might suddenly creep up again to 1%, 2% or whatever. If you take out a tracker mortgage for 5 years and in 3 years time the base rate crept up to 2%, you suddenly find yourself footing monthly mortgage payments with an 3.3% instead of 1.8% interest rate. You have to be sure that you have the flexibility to afford that.

Tracker mortgages typically allow you to 'fix out' – if during the tracker duration the interest rate keeps going up and you get cold feet, you can switch to a fixed rate mortgage. Be aware though that this fixed rate is typically around 0.5% to 1% higher compared to the tracker mortgage at any given time. Hence, the deal you get by fixing out will be worse that what you would have gotten at the start of the mortgage term when the base rate was low. It's a bit like gambling.

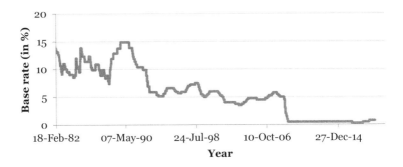

Figure 4. Bank of England base rate since the early 1980's until now (last data point is April 2019). Data from:
ttps://www.bankofengland.co.uk/boeapps/iadb/Repo.asp

Like the fixed rate mortgage, the tracker mortgage will have a period for which your 'surplus rate' (the 1.3% from our example) is guaranteed. After this, you will have to renew your deal. Periods are usually the same as for fixed rate options, typically offering a 'guaranteed' rate for 1, 2, 3, 5 or 10 years.

The **upside** of a tracker mortgage includes:

- At any given time, the interest is typically lower than for the equivalent period fixed-rate mortgage.

- You can pay off as much as you like on top of your monthly mortgage payments.

- If during the tracker period the interest rate drops, you will benefit from it – your interest will become less.

The **downside** of a tracker mortgage includes:

- If during the tracker period the interest rate goes up, you will suffer form it – you continue to pay what you signed up for, and hence will have higher monthly repayments that you can't wiggle out of.

Repayment vs. interest only

You can still choose from a repayment or interest only mortgage type for either of the options above. A repayment mortgage is the common choice, where each month you pay off both, interest and cost of the house. This means you build up 'equity' – every month, you own a little more of the house and the bank a little less. In contrast, if you have an interest only mortgage, all you pay off is the interest; the remainder of the house cost sits in a different account. Your mortgage advisor should explain both options to you and make a recommendation what you should opt for. A repayment mortgage is by far the most common choice, as it is clear what you will own when.

Mortgage interest rates

Mortgage interest rates may vary from month to month. However, the table below illustrates a basic pattern which you will find when choosing based on fixed/tracker and short/long term.

Table 16. Common pattern for mortgage interest rates of a tracker vs. fixed rate mortgage. Tracker rates for a Bank of England base rate of 0.5%.

Period (years)	Tracker	Fixed rate
1	1.8% (0.75% above base rate)	2.3%
2	2.2% (1.25% above base rate)	2.8%
3	2.6% (2.55% above base rate)	3.1%
5	3.5% (3.45% above base rate)	4.0%
10	4.5% (4.45% above base rate)	5.0%

Remember that the following main factors affect the interest rate:

- The period for which you secure the interest rate.

- Your loan-to-value ratio (see following sections).

- The type of mortgage.

Upfront fee

You often have an additional choice: you can pay an upfront fee in exchange for a slightly better interest rate, or not pay any fee. Your lender will be able to calculate the difference for you – it is often not a lot, e.g. £20 per month in mortgage repayments. If you choose to pay the upfront fee, you can add it to your mortgage; you therefore don't have to tap into your savings if you don't want to. Upfront fees are typically around £1,000.

3.4.3 Mortgage term

The mortgage term is different from the period for which you are guaranteed a certain interest rate. The mortgage term is the time it will take you to pay off your full mortgage. The calculation is not quite as simple due to compound interest, however in principle your mortgage term depends on:

- The value of the mortgage (how much you are borrowing)

- Your monthly repayments which you agreed to

- Your interest rate

Table 17. Example mortgage term and repayment schedule.

Item	£
Mortgage amount	£140,000
(Deposit	£30,000)
Monthly repayment	£1000
Interest rate over mortgage lifetime*	3.5%
Mortgage term	**15 years**

* Make a conservative estimate, rates might go up.

You will have worked out an approximate figure for both, the mortgage value and monthly repayment, in the previous chapters. Based on the previous section, you will have a rough idea what your interest rate will be – you can use 3.5% for a rough long-term estimate. Plug these three figures into a mortgage calculator, and out pops your mortgage term. You can for example use this calculator:

https://www.moneysavingexpert.com/mortgages/mortgage-rate-calculator.

The longer the mortgage term, the longer you have to pay interest on what you borrowed and hence the higher the total cost of your mortgage. It can hence be advisable to pay off as much as you can every month in order to minimise the total interest you have to pay. On the other hand, you have to balance this with what you can realistically afford. The table below shows this effect. As you can see, it is a fine balancing act between having low monthly repayments and those low repayments extending the mortgage term, which then costs you extra in interest and increases your total costs. The longer you drag it out, the more you pay in interest, which will have to be covered through your monthly repayments.

Table 18. Effect of mortgage term on the total cost of your mortgage, assuming an interest rate of 3.5% and a £160,000 mortgage.

Mortgage term (years)	Mortgage	Total interest	Total cost	Monthly repayment
5	£160,000	£14,655	£174,655	£2,911
10	£160,000	£29,890	£189,890	£1,582
15	£160,000	£45,932	£205,932	£1,144
20	£160,000	£62,768	£222,768	£928
25	£160,000	£80,382	£240,382	£801
30	£160,000	£98,752	£258,752	£719

3.4.4 Deposit and Loan-to-Value (LTV)

The loan-to-value ratio is basically the percentage of the cost of the house which the bank has to lend you. Hence, this depends on your deposit.

The calculation is as follows:

- Divide your deposit by the cost of the house

- Subtract the result from 1

For example, a £180,000 home bought with a £30,000 deposit works out like this:

- Deposit divided by cost: 30,000/180,000 = 0.167 (hence you pay 16.7% of the cost)

- 1-0.167 = 0.833 (hence the bank pays 83.3% of the cost)

- Your LTV is 0.83

The lower your LTV (and hence the lower the percentage of the home cost which your bank pays for), the better the interest rates that you will get. This is because the more of your own money you put into the property, the less risk for the bank. Have a look at the table below for an illustrative example.

The interest rate typically drops for each LTV step of 0.05 (5%). It could be important that if you are close to the threshold to get under it (e.g. getting from a 0.76 to 0.74 LTV), but there is no real point breaking your back to go from an LTV of 0.79 to 0.76 by increasing your deposit, as it usually won't affect your interest rate at all. You would only have to repay a little bit less and pay a little bit less interest as a consequence, but that's often negligible.

Table 19. Effect of loan-to-value (LTV) on interest rate. A LTV of 0.8 means that the bank pays for 80% of the house, while you pay for the remaining 20% of it. The lower the LTV, the better the interest rate. Example for illustration purposes only, although based on realistic figures.

LTV	Interest rate: 2-year fixed	Interest rate: 5-year fixed
0.95	3.51%	4.33%
0.90	2.29%	2.82%
0.85	2.07%	2.52%
0.80	2.07%	2.52%
0.70	1.98%	2.18%
0.60	1.93%	2.13%

If you look at the table above, you can also see that initially the interest rate may drop quickly with every 5% LTV that you gain. However, it tails off. Again, think whether it is worth breaking your back and putting everything you have into a deposit if you gain that extra bit in interest. For illustration purposes, consider a £200,000 property with a mortgage over 20 or 25 years:

- At **2.52% interest** (0.85 LTV, £170,000 mortgage, £30,000 deposit), your **monthly payment is £903** and your total interest cost is £46,611 **over 20 years**.

- At **2.18% interest** (0.75 LTV, £150,000 mortgage, £50,000 deposit), your **monthly payment is £772** and your total interest cost is £35,171 **over 20 years**.

- At **2.52% interest** (0.85 LTV, £170,000 mortgage, £30,000 deposit), your **monthly payment is £764** and your total interest cost is £59,326 **over 25 years**.

As you can see, a balance can be struck between deposit, mortgage term and total cost of interest to suit your lifestyle and funding.

Run a few of these calculations and ask your mortgage advisor to run through several of these scenarios together with you. That will put you in the best position to make a sensible and affordable choice that does not result in you eating tinned beans for the next 20 years.

3.4.5 Help to Buy equity loan

If you are looking at buying a new build, you may benefit from the government's Help to Buy scheme, respectively the 'Help to Buy equity loan'. This scheme in essence offers first time buyers who are struggling with their deposit up to 20% of the new build cost as a short-term loan, so that they only need to have saved up for a 5% deposit and they can get a 75% LTV mortgage interest rate.

Be aware: The 20% which the government lends you is interest free for only the first five years. If you have not paid everything back by then, you will start paying interest on it. If you proceed with the Help to Buy equity loan scheme, you have to budget for monthly repayments of both: your mortgage, and your Help to Buy equity loan. Your monthly fixed repayments will hence be higher.

You can find more information here:

https://www.helptobuy.gov.uk/equity-loan/equity-loans/.

3.4.6 Cash back

At mortgage start

Several mortgage lenders offer you cash back when you start a mortgage. This may be exclusive to customers who already have a current account with them for a certain amount of time – find out early and open one. Cash back is often in the region of £500 to £1,000, which is a nice boost when moving in and having to do small repairs. If you are lucky, you might get another £500 for e.g. being a first time buyer. This is often coupled to a poor interest rate though for a LTV of something like 0.85 or worse .

When renewing

As we have seen when looking at periods for fixed or tracker rates, you will most likely renew your mortgage arrangement during the mortgage term once the period for your agreed interest ends. At this point, a bank may offer you another cash back bonus to stay with them; this can be £50 to around £300 – again, find out. These schemes may change over the years.

3.4.7 Negative equity

As you plan your property purchase, you may hear the term 'negative equity' – typically from your surveyor or financial advisors. Negative equity means that you owe the bank more than your could sell your home for. For example, if you take out a 95% mortgage and owe the bank £190,000 for a £200,000 house, and suddenly the housing market crashes or the roof falls off, your house might only fetch £180,000. You would hence lose the difference between what you can sell the property for and what you owe the bank.

3.4.8 Finding the right mortgage lender

Now that you know all this stuff about mortgages, you might even have a lot of fun shopping around for the most competitive mortgage lenders for your needs. The three most common ways to find a mortgage are the following:

- **Mortgage broker.** You might get this as the free service offered by the agent, where a broker will already run you through the currently best options on their system. Take note of those. Remember, if you use them to get actually the mortgage, you have to pay a broker fee. No-one will stop you to approach the lender yourself though through their normal high street branches after visiting a broker for an initial chat. Just sayin'.

- **Lender websites.** Banks and building societies all have a mortgage section on their website, where you can punch in your rough figures (income to find out the maximum they would lend you; property price, deposit and mortgage term to find out their mortgage interest rates). This is a bit more involved, but gets you straight to the source of information.

- **Online comparison sites.** As for everything else, online comparison sites will give you a good first look at what is on offer for your circumstances. You can try for example:

  - https://www.moneysupermarket.com/mortgages
  - https://www.comparethemarket.com/mortgages/
  - https://www.uswitch.com/mortgages

Again, you can only use figures as guidance and make an appointment with the lender directly.

Attention: Take note of the initial fees that apply to each mortgage. A great mortgage rate might be overshadowed by a hefty fee. Also, fees on comparison websites may be higher than those straight from the lender. This might be to (partially) cover the referral fee.

Attention: Not all comparison websites may show all mortgages. Make sure you have gotten results for all major banks and building societies before making decisions.

Attention: Comparison sites may sneakily hide 'booking fees', 'arrangement fees' etc. in the mortgage offer. Read the offer terms carefully to find out whether that is the case.

3.4.9 Mortgage valuation

When offering you a mortgage, a crucial step is that your bank will carry out a valuation. Sometimes you have to pay for this, sometimes not – find out about those fees before you commit. When valuing the property, the bank will "send someone round" to check whether the property is worth what you offered to pay for it. In practice, this rather means that someone will check whether the property is worth what the bank is lending you on it. If the bank is only lending you 60% of the property price, you can hence see that a bank would feel a lot more confident recovering that compared to lending you 95% of the property price. Either way, you will never see the valuation report or the lender's valuation estimate. As everyone will tell you – do your own survey to avoid buying a property that will lose you a fortune.

You should allow 2-3 weeks between the mortgage appointment and receipt of the mortgage offer: 1 week to schedule the valuation and carry it out, and up to 2 weeks for the lender to receive and review the valuation and issue the mortgage offer (or not).

3.4.10 More info

- You can find general tips for example on 'Unbiased':

  https://www.unbiased.co.uk/

- A good source of information is moneysavingexpert.com, which hosts a number of articles covering many aspects of buying your own home:

  https://www.moneysavingexpert.com/

3.4.11 Who can help

You can find independent advisors that can help with financial decisions, mortgages and the whole home buying process (at a fee) on 'Unbiased': https://www.unbiased.co.uk.

All major banks should offer a free mortgage appointment. Book in advance and allow around 2 hours.

You can enlist the services of a mortgage broker affiliated with the agent, which is initially for free (no fee before commitment).

3.5 The property

3.5.1 Types of ownership

One of the most important things about your property is the ownership scenario. The best thing to have is a freehold property – it means you own the land the property stands on, indefinitely. In contrast, a leasehold arrangement only grants you rights to the land for a certain amount of time. Finally, there are shared ownership options, where you own part of a property – this could be either freehold or leasehold.

Freehold

If you buy a freehold property, it means you own the land that it is built on. Be aware that this still does not mean you can do whatever you want – there may be planning restrictions and the need to request planning permissions before doing any major works on the land.

There are many advantages to a freehold property:

- You will not have to pay monthly fees, such as service charges or ground rent.

- You have complete control over the property.

- You will not be bound by any terms such as restrictions on pets.

- Buying a freehold is permanent.

Sadly, if you want to buy a flat, you usually won't get a freehold. Also, many new builds come with a leasehold – be very careful when choosing this. If you are buying a regular house, it should be freehold. If it is leasehold, it is usually (much) cheaper – check whether you would in principle be able to buy the freehold for it and how much it would cost. This needs research and help from a professional to find out who owns the freehold and what the conditions and likelihood of transfer are.

Leasehold

If you buy a leasehold property, it means you buy the right to live on the land for a certain amount of time, however you do not own the land. At the end of the lease, you would have to pay to renew it or it goes back to the person it belongs to, and with it your property. If you buy a leasehold property, it should have at least 85 years left on the lease. But even then, the clock is ticking and the property will lose value the less time is left on the lease. Renewing a lease may cost 20% of the property value!

There are many disadvantages to a leasehold property:

- You will often have to pay monthly fees, such as service charges or ground rent, and are at the mercy of them changing.

- You may have to pay towards repairs to the building.

- Your property will lose value as the lease ticks down.

However, as mentioned above, leasehold properties are generally cheaper to get, and pretty much the only option if you want a flat. After all, in a block of flats, not everyone can own the same land. In return, you live in a serviced environment that may even have community facilities.

Check in great detail whether your new build (should you want one) comes with a leasehold. It's a nice little extra cash for the owner of the freehold – usually the developer – to either charge you extortionate amounts for service charges or sell the freehold to a different company that will. Also, buying the freehold off them may be ridiculously expensive. In the future, the government is expected to regulate the matter. As it stands, caution is advised.

The 'Leasehold Scandal' surrounding new builds was a big thing when it first all came to light. For articles in the news, for example check this:

- Guardian:
  https://www.theguardian.com/money/2017/jul/25/leasehold-houses-and-the-ground-rent-scandal-all-you-need-to-know

- BBC:

  https://www.bbc.co.uk/news/business-45431914

- ReallyMoving:

  https://www.reallymoving.com/blog/october-2018/leasehold-scandal

In 2017 for example, Taylor Wimpey was forced to sort out their spiralling ground rents:

https://www.bbc.co.uk/news/business-39732174

This situation on new build leaseholds / ground rents will be constantly updating (and with it hopefully the law), so do keep an eye on this if you are looking at new builds. Some developers may be more notorious for screwing their customers over than others, too.

Shared Ownership

Shared ownership is another government scheme designed for eager first time buyers who struggle with their savings and/or cash flow. You can find more details here: https://www.helptobuy.gov.uk/shared-ownership/. In essence, it lets you buy part of a property, and you pay rent on the rest of it. Long term, you are able to buy the remainder of the property depending how your financial situation improves. Have a look at the government website if this is of interest for you – there are a few conditions that you have to satisfy, and it all really depends on your personal circumstances.

3.5.2 Houses

If you choose to buy a house, you will typically get something multi-story with a garden and possibly garage and/or parking. In a house, you are able to do things such as extensions, modifications and little outbuildings (all subject to planning regulations of course). Houses come in various shapes and sizes. In general, when you search for a property, you can choose between the following general options:

- Detached

- Linked attached

- Semi-detached

- End of terrace

- Terraced

- Bungalow

Let's look at the pros and cons of these options.

Detached

A detached home does not share any walls with any other home. This means if you hate neighbours or run a 5-piece rock band, you are in for a treat.

Pros include:

- No noise from neighbour's slamming doors at 6am in the morning or partying in the living room every night.

- No shared chimney, drainpipes or other bits of the house that you have to fix jointly.

- Often space to extend the property in several directions.

- Often a garage or other storage to the side.

- Sometimes a bigger garden.

Cons include:

- Since all four sides of the house are exposed to the elements, your heating bills will be higher.

- They cost more to buy compared to equally sized attached options.

- Council tax may be higher.

- They are harder to find.

Linked detached

A link attached house is similar to a detached house, just that it is joined to a neighbour's property via a link, which is often a garage. This means that if you neighbour slams the garage shut after a night shift at 2am, you will hear it. If you run your rock band in your garage, your neighbour will hear it.

Pros include:

- Limited noise from neighbours.

- No shared chimney, drainpipes or other bits of the house that you have to fix jointly.

- Often space to extend.

- Often a garage or other storage to the side.

- Sometimes a bigger garden.

Cons include:

- Most of the house is exposed to the elements, so your heating bills will be higher.

- As detached properties, they cost more to buy compared to equally sized attached options.

- Council tax may be higher.

- The link attachment may limit what you can do without causing your neighbour to get furious.

- They are harder to find.

Semi-detached

A semi-detached property typically has one other house attached to one side. This is a very classical British building style. Strangely, the bedrooms tend to be on the side facing the neighbour, while bathrooms are on the outside and are noise isolated. Why developers came up with this idea is not quite clear.

Pros include:

- Only one neighbour to one side.

- Often a little side building / lean-to.

- Can have a side garage.

- Often potential to extend sideways.

- Reasonable amount of garden.

- Reasonable price for the size.

Cons include:

- You still got one neighbour who might have a barking dog and hoover at 5am in the morning.

- A lot of them are from the 1930s and many need a lot of TLC and repairs by now, especially roof, windows and electrics.

- You may have shared responsibilities.

- Your house is not as well protected from the elements (three exposed sides) as in a terraced house, so your heating bills will be somewhat higher.

End of terrace

And end of terrace is almost as good as semi-detached, with the catch that people slamming doors three doors down will wake you up if you are unlucky. Be aware that end of terrace homes often come under 'terraced' – you may have to do some manual searching to find them.

Pros include:

- Limited noise from neighbours – only one side is part of the terrace.

- Often potential to extend sideways.

- Reasonable amount of garden.

- Good price for the size (they usually only cost a little more than a terraced).

Cons include:

- You may have shared responsibilities.

- Your house is not as well protected from the elements as in a terraced house, so your heating bills will be a little higher.

- Noise from further down the terrace may travel up to your home through the walls.

- Not very common since every row of terraced houses has only one at each end. If you get a new build, try to score an end-terrace (unless it's adjacent to a road) – it's usually 'only' a little more expensive, maybe around 5%.

Terraced

Terraced houses can be found all over the place. You basically buy one house within a row of houses.

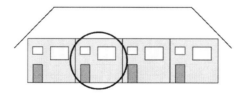

Pros include:

- Well insulated, only two sides exposed to the elements.

- Cheapest type of house.

- If you love neighbours, you'll get two sets of them.

Cons include:

- You'll have one neighbour each side.

- You may be limited in what you can do without pissing anyone off; neighbour liaison becomes a more relevant task.

- Turnover of neighbours may change the nice guy next door into a middle-aged single with a screaming Chihuahua dog cutting down your washing line during one of her drunken episodes. Remember, it's not in your control who decides to move in or out next to you.

- You can't extend the property sideways.

- You are more overlooked.

- Your garden is most likely smaller.

- Often you might only have access to on-street parking.

Bungalow

A bungalow is a single-storey house, typically build for retirees who struggle with stairs. They are very expensive for what they are. Bungalows are typically detached.

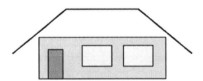

Pros include:

- No noise from your neighbours.

- No shared chimney, drainpipes or other bits of the house that you have to fix jointly.

- Often a garage or other storage to the side.

- Often a bigger garden.

- No stairs.

Cons include:

- Since all four side of the bungalow are exposed to the elements and you only have one storey, your heating bills will be high.

- They are incredibly expensive for what they are.

- Council tax may be higher.

- They are hard to find.

- They often offer less space than a detached or semi-detached alternative.

- Some may be reserved for over-60's only.

3.5.3 Flats

Everyone knows what a flat is – you basically buy a living space in a block of other living spaces.

There are some important differences between buying a flat and buying a house. If you are interested in buying a flat, have a look at the Law Society's guidance notes on buying a flat here:

https://www.lawsociety.org.uk/For.../your-guide-to-buying-a-flat-december-2015/.

The main differences to buying a house are the following:

- Different to buying a house, you don't own the land that the flat is on; you will have a leasehold, not freehold. This means that your leasehold term will tick down every year, as it does not renew when the flat is sold. The lease should be at least 85 years. You can check whether it is possible to buy a share of a freehold with other flat owners.

- In consideration of other flats, there will be more restrictions on what you can do, for example with respect to pets or making noise.

- You are most likely not directly responsible for maintenance work to the building (in contrast to buying a house) and likely won't need building insurance. On the other hand, you will have to contribute to these maintenance costs through regular ('service charge') or potentially one-off fees ('reserve fund'). Managing building maintenance is out of your hands (different to a house), so have a look whether the state of the building is decent. If it's run down, you can't do much about it.

When you are looking at flats, you should find out about the following:

- What is the lease length?

- Can the lease term be extended?

- Is it possible to buy the freehold?

- How much is the service charge?

- Is there a reserve fund and how much is it?

- What changes can I make to the flat?

- Can I have pets?

- Can I rent out part of or the whole flat?

- Is it allowed to run a business from the flat?

- If it is a retirement flat – what are the conditions if re-selling and what are other restrictions?

3.5.4 New builds

New builds come in all shapes and forms – detached, semi-detached, terraced including end of terrace and as bungalows. The difference is that – well – they are new. So you get quite a few perks with them, but there are also important factors to consider that you might not encounter when buying an older property.

First of all, there are several **benefits** to a new build:

- You get a 10-year warranty on it (make sure you do!). On the other hand, the small print may exempt certain work, and will most likely not cover things such as the quality of finishes and workmanship. Make sure this is covered through 'snagging' provisions.

- You are unlikely to have major repairs in the first few years and can budget a lot less for repair costs. If you have issues requiring major repairs, your warranty should cover this.

- You will be the first occupant and if you get there early before the home is finished (if you buy off plan or during the development stage), you have a certain amount of control over the interior design, such as the looks of kitchen and bathroom (at the minimum you can choose colour schemes).

- Energy efficiency is typically a lot better than in older properties, so your monthly running costs will be lower.

- If you want to use the Help to Buy scheme, you can do so with a new build.

However, there are also several **downsides** to a new build, including:

- You will encounter bills in the thousands for carpet fitting, curtains etc. – usually, you just buy the 'shell' of the house with ideally kitchen and bathroom fitted and walls painted. The floors will most likely be bare concrete. We saw one home with footprints of a fox or something in it, very cute.

- You may get tricked into a leasehold; be very careful.

- You may have to pay monthly service charges for the estate that could go up unchecked. Again, be very careful about what you sign up for.

- The home has not been put to the test, so you will be the first to encounter any issues. New builds can be thrown up fast and cheaply, and big issues may only show up after several years.

- When drying out, the home will most likely develop settlement cracks.

- If the contractor was in a rush to finish, you may find a lot of teething problems with your new home and you have to chase the developer to put things right.

- Gardens are usually (much) smaller.

- The home itself is usually smaller than a comparable older home, although this has been changing. You often get an en-suite that no-one needs, further reducing living space.

- Hollow walls that need special fittings and may let more noise through.

- If you buy early on, before the property is even built ('off plan'), your timeline can be very uncertain. As one builder said it: "once they got you in the net, they can do whatever they want". Remember that the developer only commits to a timeline at exchange of contracts, which is often many months after you commit to the house. Your home may be finished with a 6-12 month delay. Again, check this carefully before committing.

Good to know

Buying a new build on a mortgage will require the developer to satisfy criteria set by your mortgage lender, such as being part of the NHBC warranty scheme. Check with your lender.

Remember that you can negotiate on a new build! At minimum, you may get help with the stamp duty, solicitor fees or new carpets. See whether you can negotiate down 10% or 5%, especially if you buy one of the later homes on a less perfect plot.

In terms of warranty, you need to get clued up what to look for; speak to new build advisors about this. For example, check for a 'snagging provision', which means that the builder has to fix small things such as doors scraping over the carpet directly in the first two years. Also make sure you get a copy of warranties for all white goods.

If you are going down the new build route, have a look around show homes of the developers you are interested in early. More importantly, see whether some of their homes come up for sale after a few years. This will give you an idea how they deteriorate once the gloss has faded. We saw a 1-year old new build by a popular developer, and it had signs of a major leak and many settlement cracks throughout. Remember that the images you see when you buy a new build are (mostly) computer generated – look at their real stuff!

Buying the finished thing vs. buying off plan

In the beginning stages of a new development, you will have to commit to a purchase 'off plan'. This means that nothing has been built yet, there are just pictures and plot locations to go by. With the current race for properties, buying off plan might likely secure you the best plot. However, you have less negotiating power and you don't know what will happen to the estate. For example, if an estate is put up via a council to hit new home targets and no-one buys the stuff, you might find yourself in a new build development that is largely rented out to council tenants. That might not help the future value of your property. On the other hand, you might only have to commit around £500 to £2,000 in reservation fee at the off plan stage – if you are happy with risking to lose it in case the development takes a weird turn over the next month and/or no-one else buys there, then you should be OK.

If you buy the new build at a point where it is finished or almost finished, you know exactly what you are buying. However, many design choices might have already been made for you. On the other hand, once a developer is done with an area, they want rid of the remaining properties. This will be the best time to get a substantial discount, although the plot might be mediocre. Remember, if you get the plot that is next to a noisy road, your home will likely always sell for less than the rest of the estate.

Process

The process for buying a new build is a bit different time-wise than a 'used' home. Usually, you put down a usually £500 to £2,000 reservation fee to secure your plot. This is non-refundable. You are then expected to exchange contracts once there is a confirmed timeline on the house. Here is a bit more vocabulary for you:

- **Short-stop date**: the proposed date on which the developer thinks the home will be finished. Many properties are not finished by the date.

- **Long-stop date**: the safety margin which the developer gives himself/herself to get the home completed and give you the keys. This one is usually the more realistic outlook.

As with all properties, exchanging contracts means you have to pay 10% of the property price and are legally bound to buy it. Then you have to wait a long time for the home to actually go up before you can finally complete the purchase and move in. This is different from buying an older house, where usually a good few months go by before exchange of contract and payment of the 10% deposit while you and your solicitor conduct all checks. But it all depends on your developer, any chain and the particular circumstances of the house. Check before you commit.

Wise words of warning

Recently, many issues with new builds have come up in the media that relate to poor build quality as bad as 'pretty much the whole thing has to be re-built'. Unfortunately, it is a possibility that no-one in the new build development process actually really cares about the quality of your new home and your ultimate happiness: the building firm may want to push build completion through as cheaply as possible to get the cash, contractors who put everything together may want to see the pay check for minimum effort and cost (the builders themselves may care even less since they are so detached from the buyer) and sales staff may only be interested to get rid of stock to get the commission. So for none of these people, there is an actual reward in providing you with a quality home, aside from some costs fixing those things that you find out about. Supposedly that's still cheaper than building well in the first place.

One of the big issues flagged by BBC News in December 2018 was that of insufficient mortar being used in new homes. Obviously this takes a few years to fall apart, and according to the report, many home owners were subject to gagging orders / non-disclosure agreements, meaning that the scale of the scandal could not be fully established. The report continues to illustrate that on one estate alone, developer Taylor Wimpey agreed to replace the mortar in more than 90 properties. The full article is here:

- https://www.bbc.co.uk/news/business-46454844

It was also featured by the Sun here:

- https://www.thesun.co.uk/news/7917727/new-build-homes-taylor-wimpey-low-quality-mortar/

Large defects and issues with the build quality ultimately carry one main issue with them: massive amounts of stress and not being able to settle in your own home. Issues take a long time to resolve: you have to think months and years. Another article on BBC News illustrates this with the example of a home owner who discovered 300 faults in his £330,000 Taylor Wimpey home, ultimately requiring him to move into alternative accommodation after one year of faffing:

- https://www.bbc.co.uk/news/uk-england-norfolk-44139491

Over the last years, we have heard several horror stories about the issues that unfold once you hand over the cash for your dream new build – leaking boilers creating never before seen habitats behind plaster, whole floors and house fronts having to be re-built, 6-month delays and so on. Strangely enough, all these were houses offered by the same developer as above. So to get away from this restricted view and get a wider perspective, it will be wise to do some research:

1. Check the news.

Houses that start falling apart will ultimately make it into the news. This will give you a decent handle on the practices of the developer you are thinking about buying from. Also, if your developer just had a 5% drop in their share price and has to fix up half of their old housing stock, chances are they won't have much financial lee-way to put together a quality home for you and you might encounter massive delays. So just google something like "Developer xyz news" and see what you find. BBC News also offers insights into the company's share prices, if that is of any use to you.

2. Check Social Media and review websites.

To get a better feel for issues that crop up with developers after people have moved in, you can get a feel for the aftercare service by checking in on customer comments on social media and review websites. This will likely throw up mostly negative experiences, but you can get a feel for issues with the team in your area and the nature of the issues. Be aware that companies can hide/disable visitor comments etc, so here a few tricks:

- Facebook: look up the developer and then check the comments on their posts and/or adverts. Very enlightening.

- Twitter: same as above. Check customers' comments on Tweets sent out by the developer. And obviously search for comments with the handle.

3. Check the National New Homes Customer Satisfaction Survey.

The Home Builders Federation (NHB) releases survey data gathered from people who bought a new home something like 8 weeks after they got the keys. The survey is very comprehensive and reasonably up-to-date, with 57,972 responses for the year 2016/17. It is somewhat angled at the positive aspects of buying a new build, but you find useful statistics such as ratings for most developers and many overview statistics on how satisfied people were with more than 20 aspects of their new home. If nothing, this will help you set your expectations right. For example, 99% of respondents reported having had problems with their home which they had to report to the builder after moving in, with 69% of respondents having to report 6 or more problems. So: just expect it, problems are part of the parcel. You find the survey here:

https://www.hbf.co.uk/policy/policy-and-wider-work-program/customer-satisfaction-survey-new/

3.5.5 Build your own

This is a can of worms and warrants its own book. You basically are in charge of putting up the whole thing from scratch, to your exact specification.

From having looked into this option, it seems to cost a similar amount of money to buy land and build your own house on it than it does cost to buy an old house with the freehold. However, there are a few complicating factors before you even think about further details:

- You are unlikely to get a big mortgage on it. You may be able to borrow around 75% of the land cost and 60% of the build cost, so you need substantial savings to fund the endeavour

- The whole risk rests with you – you may lose most of your money if the builder disappears over night and you are not insured

- It can be hard to find land to buy (the 'plot'), especially in or around cities, and you need planning permission for it. You will have to look in areas that are less popular and established

- You (respectively your builders) have to sort out the whole connection to the 'grid' – water, electricity, sewage, road works etc. and chase builders, contractors and all sorts of people daily

Bear in mind, it can be done and certainly makes for an exciting project. Find detailed guidance, expert advice and input from developers on this if you wish to go down this route. To get started, have a look at the government's Self Build Portal:

https://www.ownyourhome.gov.uk/scheme/self-build-portal/

Planning permission

If you buy a plot of land, you need planning permission to build a house on it. Ideally, the plot should already have planning permission when you acquire it. Of course, plots without planning permission cost less. If you like a bit of a risk and have other things you'd be happy to do with the land, you can buy it and apply for planning permission afterwards. If a plot has lapsed planning permission, there is no guarantee you will get it again on re-application.

Insurance

Don't even consider skimping on the insurance. If you use a bigger contractor, they should have insurance against insolvency. If this is not the case, inform yourself regarding self build insurance policies and options. Make sure you really get this one right so that you don't wind up with a pile of bricks and your 10% deposit and/or other investments down the drain.

Stamp duty

Here is the good news: if you build your own house, you only pay stamp duty on the land! This may not matter in your circumstances, but if you move on to your second property, that can be a massive saving.

VAT

Here is another bonus: you can claim back all VAT that you pay on all material that go into building your own home, as long as the supplier is VAT registered. If your contractor is VAT registered, they might already charge you exclusive of VAT (remember, services including labour are not included in this). If you have to reclaim VAT yourself, you have to do a single claim comprising all your bills within three months.

Check for changes to these rules before you embark on the project to not lose out.

Get clued up

If you want to go ahead with the self build, obviously this little section is by no means enough to have the whole process figured out. Make sure you spend lots of time reading up on the topic and talking to independent experts and people who went through the process before. There are whole books, which will make a worthwhile investment.

3.5.6 Houseboats

I know! But, just for the sake of completeness, that's an option, too.

Look into it if you love freedom, water and don't need much space. You can start with this website:

https://www.waterways.org.uk/boating/buying/buying_a_boat

Chapter 4

Finding a home

4. FINDING A HOME

Now that you have a first understanding of what is involved in buying your own home, in this chapter we have a look at how to find one. The house hunting process can be confusing and take a long time. The more you work out in advance what you want and where you want to live, the easier it will be to find a property suitable for your wishes that you'll be happy with long-term. In this chapter, we hence take a look at many things that you can work out and research for yourself as well as how to find homes on the market. It covers:

- Guide questions to help you define what you want in a home and what your priorities are.

- Determining where you want to live and research you can do to examine areas.

- Research you can do to establish environmental factors (flood risk, noise, pollution...) for areas you like.

- Finding properties on the market through Rightmove and Zoopla, estate agents and other means.

- Doing your own research into the value of a property.

- Different types of sale you might encounter and the difference between a chain-free purchase and that in a chain.

Chapter 4 contents

4. FINDING A HOME..104

4.1 What do you want in a home

To begin with, it will help you a lot to draw up a list of what you are looking for in a home. You will find that there are tons of things, but that also some of them are deal breakers. Rank them, until you have a basic idea of what you are looking for with respect to size, features, work that needs doing etc. To help you, here is a list of requirements to think about:

- How many bedrooms do you want?

- Do you want a big garden, small garden or none?

- Are you prepared to do major work – central heating, electrical wiring, windows, roof?

- Are you prepared to do some work – repointing, repairs, façade rendering, internal decoration

- Do you want a big kitchen?

- Do you want lots of light through windows?

- Do you want a conservatory or potential for one?

- Do you want a garage and/or off-road parking?

- Are you OK with neighbours both sides?

- Do you want a warranty on your home?

- Do you want good energy efficiency?

- What else has always been important to you when it came to choosing where you live?

Based on your answers to these questions, you will be pointed in different directions:

If you are looking for a home that does not need any work and has warranties for the coming years for both the house structure and all big ticket items (roof, windows, boiler, electrics) while at the same time a garden is not important to you and you can make concessions on area, you might be looking for a new build.

If you are looking for a home that you can put your own stamp on, with a large garden, good transport links and lots of light, being close to a park while you don't mind neighbours, you might be looking for a Victorian terraced house.

If you are looking for a low cost property that you can refurbish completely, which has lots of potential with respect to location and space for three garages at the back but doesn't need anything but structural integrity, you might scoop up a house at an auction.

It is important when making these decisions to consider your budget:

- For any repairs, you need **cash**. If you are already pushing your deposit, you might be better off with a house that doesn't need much work. This will cost more to buy, but you can cover that with the mortgage.

Draw up a list with your priorities, and start having a look for options on the market. Are your expectations given your budget constraints realistic? What can you compromise on? Shortlist a few houses and have a look at them to get a first idea what you get for your money.

4.2 Where do you want to live

4.2.1 Basic area features

One of the hardest things to figure out when getting started on a property search is WHERE to search. You may already know your town or city well and know exactly where you want to live. You might have relocated a year ago and know exactly where you don't want to live. If you decided on an area, then you are already good to proceed – the next step for you is to find properties in that area that match your budget and to work out compromises. If you have no idea which area you should buy in, read on.

To shortlist potential areas, ask yourself questions about what the area should offer, and what is important to you. This can include:

- Do you want access to a train station?

- Do you want access to other public transport?

- Do you want to be close to nature or parks?

- Are you happy to live next to a busy road or do you want a side street or cul-de-sac?

- Do you want to be close to good schools?

- Are you comfortable living in an area with lots of social housing?

- Do you want to have a short commute?

- Do you need access to the motorway?

- What kind of crime do you not want to be around?

- How close do you want to be to places where you spend time (maybe you take dancing classes, learn to paint, have a regular cooking group)?

- Do you want any public offerings, such as pubs, gym, library or shops close-by? How close – walking distance, cycle ride, bus trip, and train ride?

Once you have decided on these questions, you can get to work to narrow down areas.

As a first step, if you have requirements regarding proximity to for example transport or places of leisure, you can simply draw a circle around them on a map, the radius being the distance you are willing to be away. Have a look where circles overlap or are close together.

As a second step, you can highlight areas on a map that offer the features you are looking for – parks, good schools, maybe hipsters or young entrepreneurs. This takes us to the next section – how do you find out more details about an area that go beyond infrastructure? You have to look at local area statistics (see Section 4.2.2. below).

No-goes

When you are drawing up a list of area characteristics that you are keen on, it is also important to have a think about your absolute no-goes. We have seen beautiful new build developments put up next door to a giant landfills and amazing detached houses plonked directly under major power lines. So when you think about your no-goes, consider for example:

- Power lines

- Landfills/skips

- Factories

- Phone masts

- Airports

- Incinerators

- Large schools (oh yes, you might not get out of your street in the morning)

- Hospitals (your road may turn into a car park)

- Cricket grounds (your garden may be frequented by drunks)

- Music venues

- Bars/pubs

All of the above may or may not cause you concern and you may in fact desire some of them. But make sure you check the area and street where you want to buy for those that do cause you concern.

4.2.2 Local area statistics

This is one of the big research projects when house hunting. You can piece together quite a good idea of what an area is like by investigating a variety of resources online. You can use the following websites, amongst others:

Mouseprice

On the face of it, mouseprice.com offers your standard information – sold house prices, context of other prices close-by, street view etc. However, dig a bit deeper, and you find an awesome heat-map feature that illustrates the following based on your selection:

- Average prices (median current value)

- Crime

- Burglaries

- Cost per square meter

- Social housing

Now you can get to business! All these metrics are an indirect indicator of the quality of life of an area. You can access this feature here:

https://www.mouseprice.com/property-for-sale/map

You have to register for free in order to access these heat maps. It is definitely worth it.

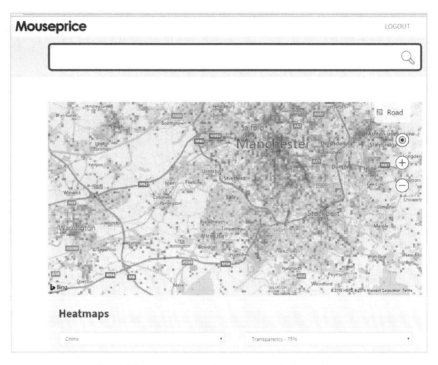

Figure 5. Screenshot of the Mouseprice heat map tool, here showing crime as selected in the drop-down menu. ©mouseprice.com

StreetCheck

Another way to learn more about the area you want to move to is streetcheck.co.uk. Punch in your postcode, and it will return the following information:

- General area information

- Type of housing

- People

- Culture

- Employment

- Crime

- Nearby

- Broadband

From here, you can have a look whether the community and social environment you would move into suits your lifestyle. Is 75% of crime violent/sexual? Maybe go elsewhere, unless you want to practice your martial arts skills. Are 90% of people full-time students? Have a think whether you like to be embedded within a rental environment or whether you prefer to move somewhere where you may become part of an established community. The information here is limitless. Be aware that it usually refers to one bigger general area – you may not get information for the specific street or surrounding streets.

You can access the website here:

https://www.streetcheck.co.uk/

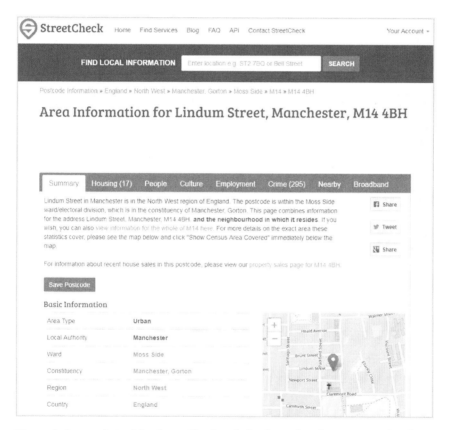

Figure 6. Screenshot of the StreetCheck website, here showing an example of an overview search result for a street (Lindum Street in Manchester). Clicking on the tabs will reveal detailed information about Housing, people, culture, employment, crime, nearby and broadband. ©streetcheck.co.uk

Office for National Statistics

This 'nomis' service is a good resource to supplement your search on StreetCheck, although some information is likely duplicate. The topics covered in great detail are:

- Who we are (Area demographics)

- How we live (Household characteristics)

- What we do (Occupations in the area)

You can access nomis here:

https://www.nomisweb.co.uk/

Nomis may cover a slightly different areas compared to SteetCheck, and you can't search by street name; have a look at the drawn areas for which both are reporting.

Figure 7. Screenshot of the nomis website, here showing an example of an overview search result for a postcode (M14 4BH). Scrolling down will reveal detailed tables about many aspects of 'Who we are', 'How we live' and 'What we do'. ©nomisweb.co.uk

4.2.3 Visit the areas

Once you have shortlisted potential areas, the best thing is to go there and walk around. Do this at different times: on working days during work time and after work as well as at the weekend in the morning, afternoon and evening/night. See who walks around, what the energy is like, how friendly people are, what is going on. You can even ask people in the street what it's like to live there, if you have the courage. If you see burnt out cars, move on.

4.2.4 Drive around to mark nice roads

What we found one of the most useful Saturday afternoons spent was driving round interesting areas and marking nice roads on a map. You can mark those that you don't like red, and those that you do like green. Just print out the bit of the map covering the area and get a highlighter out. You will start to see streets or areas where search is pointless: for example, if you are looking for a semi-detached, you will find areas that only have terraced housing. Short-listing streets like that can save you a lot of time attending unnecessary viewings and focus on areas where you'd like to buy. At the same time, you develop a feeling for different areas and what you really like in terms of surroundings.

Google maps will of course give you a good idea of the basic housing through its satellite feature. If you zoom in, you can make out whether a certain area contains only terraced housing or has semis; whether there is off-street parking; what the garden sizes are like etc.

Figure 8. Google maps satellite view, showing semi-detached houses in the left half and terraced houses over on the right. You can check out an area and shortlist streets where the type of house that you are after can be found. ©Google

4.3 Environmental factors

Other than people and facilities that you will be surrounded by, it is also important to consider environmental factors. Here are some important ones, which you can also check for yourself:

4.3.1 Flood Risk

If your property is in a flood risk zone, this is likely to impact on your mortgage and drive up your insurance premium (if you get it insured at all). You can check whether your property is in a flood risk area here:

https://flood-map-for-planning.service.gov.uk/

This government site gives you a detailed map and legend, allowing you to check for flood risk before you even make an offer.

Figure 9. Screenshot of the flood risk map tool, here showing an example of an overview search result for an area in Manchester. ©gov.uk

4.3.2 Pollution

There are a couple of websites offering real-time or day-to-day pollution maps, however these are quite coarse. For example, you can consult the Department for Environment, Food and Rural Affairs (DEFRA) **UK Air service** here:

https://uk-air.defra.gov.uk/forecasting/locations?q=b30%203rg

You can also have a detailed look at the **National Atmospheric Emissions Inventory** here:

http://naei.beis.gov.uk/data/gis-mapping

This website lets you search for several pollutants. Nitrogen Oxides (NO$_2$) are often a proxy for pollution from roads.

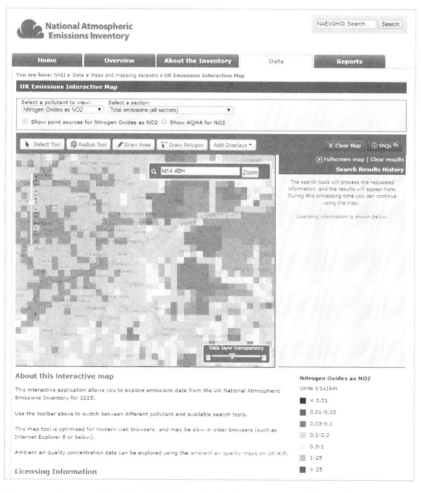

Figure 10. Screenshot of the NAEI's emission heat map tool, here showing an example search result for Nitrogen Oxides for a wider area in Manchester. ©http://naei.beis.gov.uk

If you want to dig deeper, you can explore the EarthSense project MappAir, which was also featured by the BBC:

https://www.earthsense.co.uk/mappair

https://www.bbc.co.uk/news/science-environment-42566393

The information is – at the time of writing – still clumsy to access, but keep an eye on it.

4.3.3 Noise

Believe it or not, there are also maps for noise. Have a look at for example Extrium's service here:

http://www.extrium.co.uk/noiseviewer.html

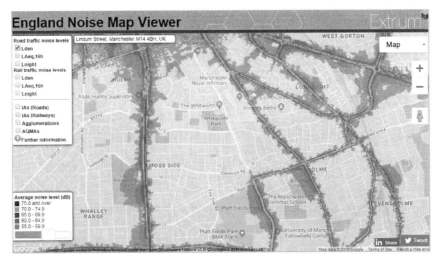

Figure 11. Screenshot of Extrium's noise map, here showing an example search result for an area in Manchester. ©extrium.co.uk

If you like data, you can also have a look at DEFRA's raw noise data here:

https://www.gov.uk/government/publications/open-data-strategic-noise-mapping

Often, noise is a direct result of major roads or railways. So if you see a nice house right next to a main road or railway, expect there to be noise. The data might not always pick up all noise in an area, especially if it is not constant. So it's still important to drive to the area at different times to make sure there are no nasty surprises.

4.3.4 Restrictions on actions

This is a harder one to research and may only come out during your solicitor's searches. However, be aware that there may be restriction on what you can do, for example for:

- Tree preservation orders

- Listed building

- Conservation areas

You can see whether talking to the estate agent already reveals such a restriction.

4.3.5 Council planning implications

Before you make an offer, it can be worthwhile to check whether the council is planning on building a new road at the end of your back garden. This is especially important if the property is located in an area that is not fully developed. You can have a look for current planning applications on the website of your local council. To find this, google something like *name of your council* and *planning portal* or *planning applications* or *planning permissions*. For Manchester for example, you end up here:

https://secure.manchester.gov.uk/info/200074/planning/5865/planning_permission

If you can't find the site, give your local council a ring and ask. Say that you want to view current planning applications in your area and where to find that. They should be able to help you out.

4.4 Area or size?

The two sections above bring us to an important question: What is more important: the area or size of the house?

You won't get both, unless you have a lot of money. So have a think about your priorities. If you are willing to compromise on area, it might be worth renting in the chosen neighbourhood for a while to find out whether that actually works for you. If you are willing to compromise on space, it might be worth locking up and not using your third bedroom for a while to see what it feels like. Any change to your current living style might hit you harder than you think; try to de-risk it so that you don't move somewhere where you will become unhappy.

4.5 How to find properties on the market

4.5.1 Online

The most common way to find properties is to search online. You can set alerts for specific search criteria, which helps a lot in staying on top of things. The most common websites are:

- Rightmove.co.uk

- Zoopla.co.uk

Both list largely the same properties, as they scrape the data from estate agents. But there are small differences between what the two websites offer.

When you get started, have a look how long properties in your area hang around on the market. Do they sell within days? Do they not sell for weeks or months? Are many reduced? This will give you a good idea how quick you have to act and how much competition you will have. Generally, it's good to have some interest in an area, as it means that it should be easy to sell the property on again. It also means of course that you will have to make a better offer than everyone else.

Rightmove

Rightmove lets you search by specific criteria, letting you shortlist properties you like and offering alerts that you can customise. You can draw specific search areas, or search by radius. Be aware that if you draw a search area, do so generously; else you might miss a property at the boundary. Rightmove has information about the house and information about the area. When you click on a property, you typically find

- Description

- Floor Plan(s)

- Map & Street View

- SchoolChecker

- Market Info

- Recent sales and similar properties

You can also look for other houses in the region, recently sold house prices in the region and the cost of properties that are sold subject to contract (called 'STC').

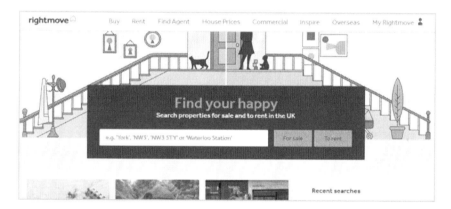

Figure 12. Screenshot of Rightmove's landing page. ©rightmove.co.uk

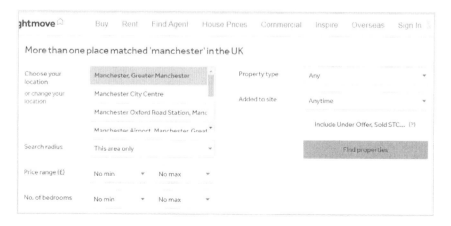

Figure 13. Screenshot of Rightmove's basic search facility, where you can specify what you are looking for. ©rightmove.co.uk

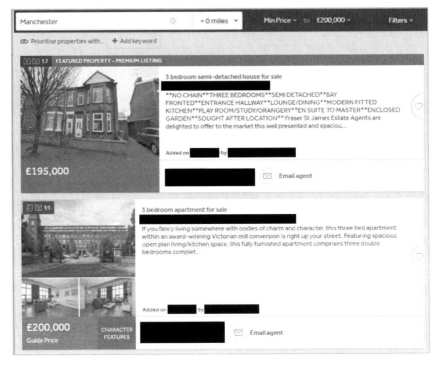

Figure 14. Screenshot of search results in grid view on Rightmove.
©rightmove.co.uk

Figure 15. Screenshot of Rightmove's personal account options (you need to sign in to use them), including alerts, saved properties, drawn areas and other options. ©rightmove.co.uk

Zoopla

Zoopla lets you search by specific criteria, letting you shortlist properties you like and offering alerts that you can customise. It has a smoother drawn area feature and has additional information for each property you are looking at, providing an estimate of the cost of bills. In addition, when you sign in, you have the option to hide properties that you are not interested in. When you click on a property, you typically find:

- Features (summary)

- Description

- Floor plan

- Map

- Price History

- Running costs estimate

- Recent sales and similar properties

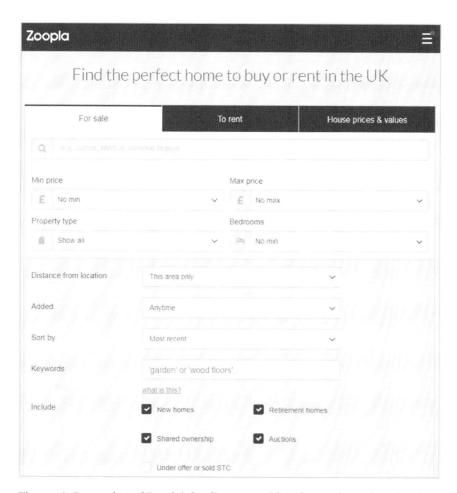

Figure 16. Screenshot of Zoopla's landing page with 'Advanced search options' expanded. ©zoopla.co.uk

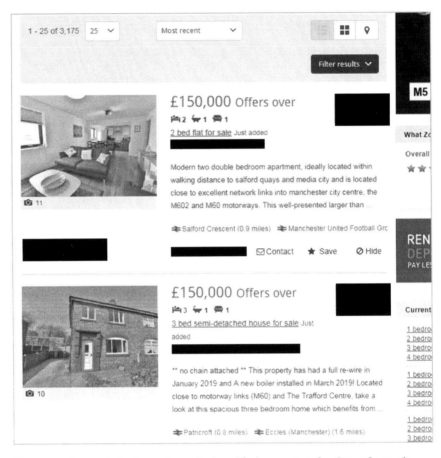

Figure 17. Screenshot of search results in grid view on Zoopla. ©zoopla.co.uk

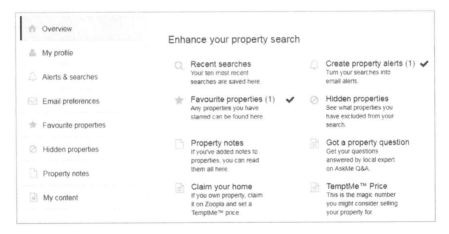

Figure 18. Screenshot of Zoopla's personal account options (you need to sign in to use them), including alerts, saved properties, drawn areas and other options. You can also hide properties. ©zoopla.co.uk

Setting alerts

Whichever provider you end up using, make sure you set up alerts. You can do this with both. Alerts allow you to exactly specify what type of property you are looking for and then get automated emails whenever an agent adds a fitting property to the market. You can set the frequency to anything, between immediate and once every week. Make sure you get alerts frequent enough that the house is still on the market by the time you ring up – in some areas, you may need to view within days in order to get a chance, whereas in other areas houses can hang around for weeks and months. Get a feel for this – better dealing with a few more emails than missing out on your dream home.

4.5.2 Agents

As mentioned in Chapter 3. , you can get on the estate agent's property alert list based on your preferences. In an ideal scenario, your agent will have you on the radar when they get new properties joining the market and send you an alert. In reality, the success of this approach varies and is dependent how 'hot' an area is. If you buy in an area where houses get snapped up fast, the agent might not have any incentive to alert you. If the agent needs to do work in order to sell, they are much more likely to keep you updated.

It certainly doesn't do any harm to be enlisted with agents, and you already get to know them a little. If you are lucky, your agent might take you on a little 'tour' round several properties in one go, and show you wild card properties you were initially not looking for. This is all good to expand your horizon and compare what you can get.

4.6 What is it worth

4.6.1 Current market value

A property is worth what someone is prepared to pay for it. Sadly, in the regular property market there are no bargains to be had. However, it is definitely worth sanity checking the property's valuation in context of the market and sales in the surrounding area. This will be a good anchor to base an offer on, and also a good way to set your expectations.

There are a couple of ways to check what roughly a property is worth, as described in the following.

HM Land Registry Open Data

All sales that go through will be logged on the HM Land Registry database, which is free for you to view:

http://landregistry.data.gov.uk/app/ppd.

On here, type in the postcode or street where you would like to buy. You can also set the earliest and latest sold date. Since results are not very logically sorted, it may be useful to set the earliest sold date to say five years back and leave the last sold date blank. If you go back in time too much, you'll just get depressed seeing how much prices have increased. If you go back too little, you won't get a feel of where the area is going.

Figure 19. Screenshot of the Land Registry's sold house prices search landing page. ©gov.uk

Looking at results will give you a first feel for how much properties of the kind you are interested in sell for. Check:

- How much the most recent purchases (dating a year or less back) went through for

- How the price changed over the years

Now you have a first idea. If the asking price of your property is £210,000, but three houses sold in the last six month for £180,000, chances are the agent is trying it on and you have room to negotiate down. Sold house prices are one of your best arguments in a negotiation. And don't let the agent tell you that there is something special about your particular house that inflates its value, they say that for all houses. Use your sound judgement. If of course the previous sales were all houses that needed a full refurb and your house already has a new roof and kitchen, then the price might of course be higher.

Zoopla

Next, we can get into a little more detective work. Head over to Zoopla. Here, you find most current property listings, but also historical ones.

As a first step, have a look at the **Zoopla property value heat maps** here:

https://www.zoopla.co.uk/heatmaps/

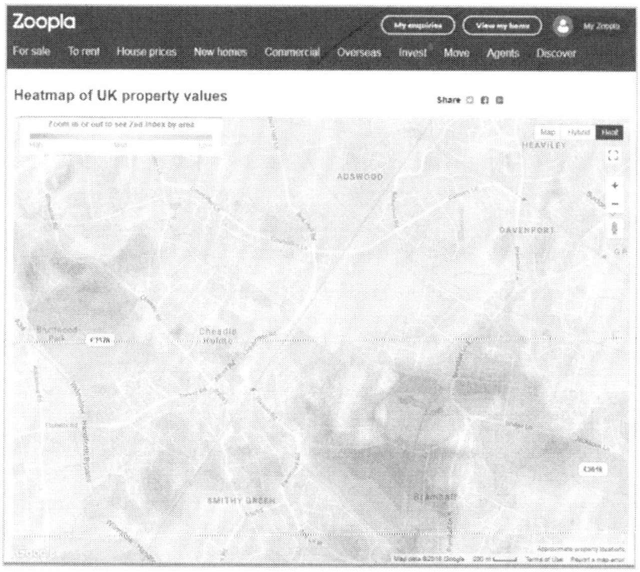

Figure 20. Screenshot of Zoopla's sold house prices heat map. ©zoopla.co.uk

Zoom into the area that you want to buy in. You will start to see patterns of where prices are high and low. Be aware that this is based on Zoopla's Zed-index, which is an estimate of value, rather than actual prices. But nonetheless, it gives you an idea what rough price idea might be realistic.

Next, have a look at current prices, sold prices and historical listings, which you can access by expanding property details.

First of all, check **how much properties in your area are on the market for**. You can put your basic search in here: https://www.zoopla.co.uk/for-sale/, just limit it to a small search radius as else it will get too convoluted to compare. Expand the search options and put in the following:

- A max price around 10% or so above what you want to pay (you might negotiate it down).

- Your property type.

- Minimum number of bedrooms (beware, some 3-beds that has the box room converted to a 2-bed run under 2-bed).

- Distance from location: this area only (or a bid wider).

- Added: anytime.

- Include: tick only 'under offer or sold STC' (subject to contract).

Hit 'Search', then click on the little map symbol to show the location of properties on a map (it's a little location pin symbol, the one on the right in the image below).

Now, zoom into the area you are interested in, and have a look how much properties are on the market for. It doesn't matter if they are sold STC, as these are all fairly recent sales. Have a look what the asking price for properties compared to yours are like.

Next, more detective work: have a look what **properties in the area actually sold for and what their asking price was**. For this, head over here:

https://www.zoopla.co.uk/house-prices/

where you find sold house prices and an archive of old adverts. Again, put in your street name or area postcode, then search. On the results page, sort by 'Last sale'. Similar to the Land Registry Open Data tool, you will get a list of past sold prices and the date of the sale. Take a note. Now, for some properties, you get the property history with it. Click on the symbol with the 'H – Property History' to see the archived marketing material.

Be aware that the agreed price for a property might initially have been higher than the sold price, as it might have been dropped following survey. Also, have a look how properties compare in terms of size and maintenance. A house with a new roof will naturally fetch more than one with an old one.

Rightmove

You can conduct a similar search on Rightmove. For properties on the market and sold STC, head over here:

https://www.rightmove.co.uk/property-for-sale.html.

Put in your area, refine your search, tick the box 'Include Under Offer, Sold STC...' and off you go. As on Zoopla, you can show properties in map view and zoom in on interesting regions. Once you are done with research and want to look for properties actually on the market, just un-tick the 'Include Under Offer, Sold STC...' in 'Filters' at the top.

For sold house prices, head over to:

https://www.rightmove.co.uk/house-prices.html

Put in your street details and click 'Map view'. Pick the correct area and period (say last 5 years) and click 'Find sold prices'. This will give you sold prices, but not the advertised price. On the other hand, it will give you an indication similar to heat maps if you zoom out.

For most properties that you save to your shortlist on your Rightmove account, you will be able to follow what happens to them after they are sold STC. Revisit old adverts a few months later. For some, you will see the actual sold price (as per Land Registry) in the 'Market info' tab once it went through. If you search over a longer time period, this can also help you calibrate how you should pitch your offer.

4.6.2 Future value

No-one will know the future value of your property. You can only do a rough guess based on its historical and recent increase in value where it might go. Since the market crashed in 2008, it has recovered and for years now topped previous prices. As of mid-2018, the average house price (Figure 21) in the UK is £228,384 – this includes houses of all sizes and those sold in London. At the same time, you can also see that it took around 8 years for house prices to recover their value which they had just before the crash. For any particular region, this might of course be different! For example, prices in a major city would have been affected differently to prices in rural communities. Since late 2013, prices have risen every year by around 3% to 10%. You can see in Figure 22 that current prices are not rising massively, with a slight downward trend. The market has been volatile in 2018, with house prices almost plateauing (no change in price over previous year). Have a look at the news what the situation is, as this might change from month to month while Brexit uncertainty and other factors are impacting on the market.

Looking at these figures, you can see that over many years, you can expect the price of your property to go up if it tracks the general market. What exactly happens to the future value will depend on your exact local area: some areas might go up a lot, others might even go down. If the housing market crashes again, chances are your property will lose value, at least in the short term. Again, the extent to which this happens will depend on the local area.

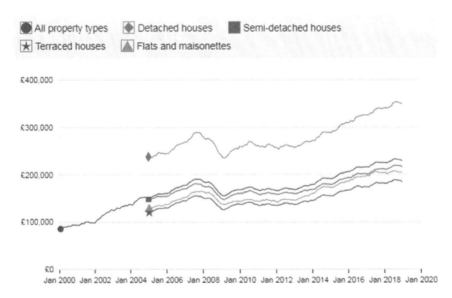

Figure 21. Average house prices in the UK since 2000. Data source: http://landregistry.data.gov.uk/app/ukhpi.

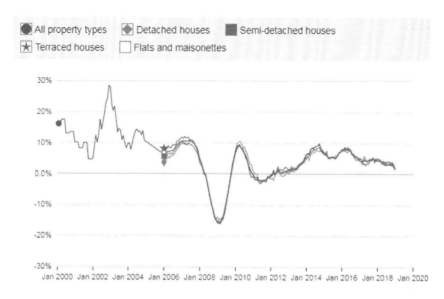

Figure 22. Change in house prices compared to the previous year for the whole of the UK since 2000. Shown are data for all property types (from 2000) and types broken down by detached, semi-detached and terraced since 2006. Data source: http://landregistry.data.gov.uk/app/ukhpi.

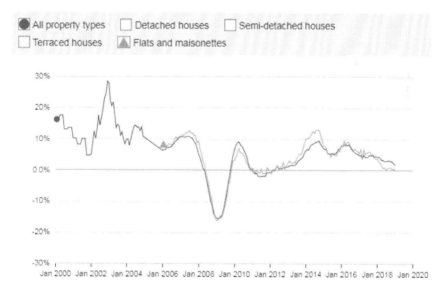

Figure 23. Change in flat prices compared to the previous year for the whole of the UK since 2000. Shown are data for all property types (from 2000) and flats/maisonettes since 2006. Data source: http://landregistry.data.gov.uk/app/ukhpi.

Local areas do experience boom and bust periods. There maybe years where property prices shoot up by £10k, £20k or £30k – maybe investors got wind of the area, maybe something is being built that encourages buyers. Keep an eye open for local developments, and try to find out in which area houses sell well. In the end, what you also want to know is that the property will sell again if you ever want to get rid of it.

You can do a more local area search using the Land Registry UK House Price Index:

http://landregistry.data.gov.uk/app/ukhpi

You can compare trends of your area to those of the whole country by clicking into the table on 'Compare with location...'.

Zoopla and Rightmove also both offer 'stats' on price trends. These are more local than the ones described above. Have a look at these, but regard them with caution. They are usually lagging behind, as an up- and coming area might have already shot up by the time sales go through and data become available. However, do have a look at the value change for your local area, and see how it compares with the national average. Make sure you select the correct property type, for example a semi-detached, to get a more precise estimate.

4.6.3 More info

- You can find the Land registry here:

  https://www.gov.uk/government/organisations/land-registry

4.7 What is the sale type?

4.7.1 Estate agent

This is the most common way of buying, still. The process is the following:

- You book a viewing with the agent.

- The agent shows you round the house; the owner may or may not be there. Sometimes, the owner might show you round, but that is far less common.

- If you like it, you might want to come back for a second viewing.

- You make an offer to the agent.

- The agent will lead the negotiation between you and the vendor.

- The agent may ask for best and final offers or sealed bids if several buyers compete for the same property.

- The agent will give you feedback whether your offer was accepted or declined.

When you put in an offer and start negotiating, you should receive feedback within 24-48 hours. If you don't hear back for days, the agent might use your offer to drive up someone else, Make sure to manage this; you can request feedback if you have not heard back after 2 days or withdraw your offer.

4.7.2 Purplebricks or similar (self-marketing)

Purplebricks is one of the options through which homeowners can self-market their home. They typically get assistance from an independent local estate agent, who will help them in selecting the buyer (and drive up the price). The process is the following:

- You book a viewing through the online portal.

- In most cases, the owner shows you round the house.

- You make an offer to the vendor through the online portal.

- The vendor will accept or decline your offer, and you can change your offer; there is facility to exchange brief notes. This is a bit like bidding on eBay, and you have to be careful not to get carried away.

- The agent will help the vendor select the best buyer and may set one or several rounds of best and final offers.

- The online portal will inform you whether your offer was ultimately successful.

Our experience with Purplebricks was that the viewings were quite informative as they were often accompanied by the vendor. However, the agent involved in the sale manipulated sales into a bidding war and on one property called best and final offers twice. It was our feeling that these Purplebricks houses sold for more than they were worth. But this might have been specific to our region. You will find out for yourself once you can compare these offerings to conventional sales.

4.7.3 Auction

If you don't mind work and risk, buying at auction might be an interesting option. Houses wind up at auction for different reasons – they may have been repossessed, unoccupied for ages or given to the auction house by people who inherited them. Hence, the state they are in varies widely, which should be reflected in the price.

You may find auction houses listed on Rightmove and Zoopla. Rightmove lets you filter for auction properties once you entered your basic search and view results in list view, although this will also return all 'Modern Method of Auction' properties (see section below). Find out about your local auction houses and get their listings directly from them. You should be able to view the properties. Make sure to get as much information as possible from the agent, and ideally neighbours.

Contrary to a normal sale, there are things you can (should) do IN ADVANCE of bidding for an auction property:

- Request all legal information from the seller's solicitor. Have a look at Chapter 8.3.1 what this should contain. It may also contain the Searches (below).

- Carry out searches. Jump to Chapter 8.3.2 to see what a solicitor would look for. You can request most of these yourself, but you may need help with interpreting them. Searches may already be included in the property's legal pack.

- Get advice from a solicitor and consider carrying out a survey.

- Make sure your mortgage lender would give you a mortgage on the auction property and find out what their terms are.

- Be aware that guide- and reserve price may change on auction day.

Buying a property at auction means that the moment you win the bid, you enter a binding agreement for it. Hence, you need to be sure that you want it. Different to the normal sales process, if you buy at auction, things happen fast:

- On auction day, you have to put down the 10% deposit immediately. You basically fast-forward to exchange of contracts in a split second. You will also pay an admin fee to the auction house, possibly around £200 to £300.

- Within 28 days (or possibly 20 working days), you are expected to complete and pay the remainder of the price. Make sure your mortgage is ready to go before you even raise your hand.

Be aware that once you win the auction bid, the risk of the property rests with you. So if there is something dodgy about it or a disgruntled auction looser tips off the council about structural issues, you will have to deal with the fall-out. Also be aware that you will lose everything you spent on examining the property if someone else bids more than you and you don't win.

If you buy a property at an auction, you actually have to show up and raise your hand. Make sure you find out about auction dates early so that you can check out the available properties with sufficient time. Maybe attend an auction just to get a feel for this before you go to actually bid.

4.7.4 Modern Method of Auction

This method is different from the conventional auction, in that you can view and vet the property for sale and then bid online through the agent or another facilitator. It's a bit like eBay. The property will likely be on the books of an Estate Agent, although the bidding process is online. The Modern Method of Auction quite frankly appears like a new attempt to drive up prices, since people bid from the word 'go' as they would do on eBay. Be aware that the listed **guide price** is unlikely to be the lowest price which the seller is willing to accept. Rather, it's a starting point, like your £1 eBay listing. The minimum acceptable price is termed the **reserve price** – typically 10% more than the guide price. If you engage in the process, be sure that you know your limits and do your research on what the property is worth. It will be easy to get attached and wanting to win, and may lead to you overpaying on a property and hence throwing money into the bin. With this style, also enquire regarding requirements of the sale – for example, you may be expected to complete within 28 days. You will also be expected to put down a huge deposit from the moment you win, often 10% of the sales price – so you don't have that layer of protection offered by the conventional purchase process, where you only enter a binding agreement at exchange of contracts after several weeks or – rather more common – months.

4.7.5 Chain vs. chain free purchase

If you buy a property, it will matter whether it is in a 'chain' or not. A chain means that the vendor of the property makes the sale contingent on finding an onward purchase. If he/she is buying from another vendor who also needs an onward purchase, it can get messy. Avoid long chains, as they are a big risk – if one property doesn't work out, the whole thing might collapse and you lose everything you've spent on solicitor, surveyor etc. The time from having an offer accepted to actually moving in when you are in a chain can take ages – make sure you find out rough timeframes before committing anything. If it is just one or two people in the chain, it should be a lot less nerve-wrecking and time consuming.

If you do go forward with a property that is in a chain, the best thing to do is agree a moving plan with your vendor when your offer has been accepted. Also, make sure to minimise your costs and risks until there is certainty on the vendor's onward purchase or alternative plans. This can include:

- The vendor committing to moving into rented accommodation should he/she not be able to move out within a defined timeframe. This may not have any legal standing though unless locked in at exchange of contracts, and by that time you will have already lost a lot of money and time. Discuss with your solicitor.

- You choosing a solicitor that does not charge any legal fees if your purchase falls through. Remember, you will still be expected to cover the costs of searches.

- You holding off all solicitor activities, searches and survey after engaging the solicitor (instruct your solicitor to "hold fire") until the vendor found an onward purchase and you are happy with any associated risks and potential delays, especially if your vendor is buying into a chain (may fall through) or a new build (can be delayed by up to one year).

- You continuing to look at alternative properties until there is clarity on the timeline of your chosen property. Remember, until your solicitor and surveyor get to work, all you lose is around £300 solicitor deposit. If your solicitor is nice, they will apply this deposit to your next purchase and not just scoop it up and show you the door.

A chain-free purchase is often the best option. This typically means that the house is already empty and that the vendor is motivated to sell it. Either someone died, or the vendor already moved out. Possibly, the vendor is planning to move abroad or it might also be an ex-student house which is being sold off. Just expect it to not always be as flashy as a home someone is still living in. Most likely, the furniture is already out and decoration is not great. Look past that – once the vendor in a chain with the amazing interior design decor taste has removed all furniture, all houses likely look a bit dire.

Chapter 5

Getting stuff ready for an offer

5. GETTING STUFF READY FOR AN OFFER

In this Chapter, we have a look at things you should consider preparing once you get close to the offer stage. Once you offer on a property, things might go very fast: your offer might be accepted within a few days, and you suddenly have to produce a lot of documentation regarding your finances and identity. Getting these prepared early will take the stress out of the process and avoid you scrambling for payslips while the home remains on the market. We will take a look at the following:

- Getting an Agreement in Principle.

- Writing a 'pitch' for the offer stage.

- Collecting evidence which you will likely be asked to produce.

- Lining up a solicitor early.

Chapter 5 contents

5.1 Agreement in principle (mortgage)

At the point of making an offer, most agents expect you to have an 'Agreement in Principle'. This means that you have basically run with a bank through your affordability, and based on your personal circumstances, the bank confirms that they will lend you a certain amount. Not all banks do this anymore, but most of them will.

The way you get an Agreement in Principle is direct through most mortgage lenders (unless you want to get one through a broker). You don't have to later use them for your actual mortgage. However, be aware that each time you get an Agreement in Principle, there will be a 'hard' footprint on your credit score. No-one knows whether this really matters; the general consensus is that it is wise not to have too many of them in a short space of time. So get this document at a point where you think you are going to put in an offer. An Agreement in Principle is typically valid for 3 to 6 months.

Remember that an Agreement in Principle does not guarantee a mortgage. It is a rather superficial check of your resources and ability to pay back a loan.

Online

To get an Agreement in Principle from a lender you are already banking with, it might be as simple as an online form which you have to complete. You should get the result immediately, and the whole process may only take 30 minutes. You might also be able to obtain this if you are not already a customer, but you might have to provide extra information.

In person

If there is no online option, you might have to attend an appointment, in which case you have to plan ahead more and allow time. For appointments, you might also have to bring the evidence listed below, basically:

- One month's current account statement (most recent).

- Three months' payslips (most recent).

- ID.

- Proof of address.

For an Agreement in Principle, you should have a rough idea how much you are asking for. If you get one for £250,000 and give that to the agent who has a house on the market for £200,000, it might be hard to negotiate, since you can't really say that you can't afford it.

5.2 A pitch that you are perfect buyers

Draft a pitch about who you are and why you are perfect buyers, which you can provide to the agent when making an offer. This should include information about yourself that ticks the boxes of what the agent is looking for while also making you more memorable. You could include the following information:

- That you have jobs and what you do

- That you have an agreement in principle and deposit

- That you are an 'easy mover' (e.g. living in rented with 1-month notice)

- That you have no chain

- Why you want to move in the area

This pitch could read for example like this:

> *"We are a couple looking to move to Darvesley to live closer to work and friends and settle down. Andy is a full-time regulatory lead at a chemical plant. Laura is a full-time lecturer at university. We have an Agreement in Principle for our mortgage and saved up a sufficient deposit. We have no chain, currently living in rented accommodation with a 1-month notice period. We are first time buyers and are looking forward to hearing from you."*

Boxes ticked:

- You both have good jobs.

- You have good motivation to move and see it through.

- You have the funds and can get a mortgage.

- You have no chain and can move fast, making this low risk and easy to manage.

Something like this should make you a very attractive buyer, and it will give you negotiating power. Don't lie, obviously. Just sell yourselves in the best possible light.

5.3 Evidence

Pretty much everyone whom you deal with in the house buying process will ask for the evidence below, which you can prepare as a little pack. This saves time and stress scrambling for pay slips and bank statements last minute.

5.3.1 Deposit

You need to demonstrate proof that you have the deposit in the bank which you claim to own. For this, print out a bank statement for each of your accounts (if you have several). In the printout, your ID, bank account details and the total for each of your accounts should be obvious. Screenshots of your online bank account may also be sufficient.

If you don't do online banking, request a printout from your local branch. This may take a day or more, hence allow time for this. Banks may not provide a printout of your account at short notice. Remember to take your ID.

Some stakeholders may also ask to see one or two months' worth of account statements to check what goes in and out of your main bank account. You can print this (or request it in branch) while you are already at it.

5.3.2 Employment / payslips

Typically, your last three months' payslips are required as evidence of employment and your earnings. If you don't have digital copies that you can print off, make sure you have them as hard copies on file. If you have lost your payslips, it might take a week (and cost money) to retrieve replacements from your employer. Hence plan for this early.

5.3.3 Current address

As with most proof-of address requests, most commonly any of the below will suffice. Typically, stakeholders want to see at least two items from this list:

- Council Tax Bill

- Energy Bill

- Water Bill

- Bank statement addressed to your home

- HMRC letter

- Other official communication

Make sure that you have such post go to your current address in case you recently moved.

5.4 Line up a solicitor

In chapter 3.2.3 we looked at finding a solicitor, and by the time you get to make an offer, you should have a good idea whom you would like to use. Ideally, you will have your comparison table filled in to make an informed choice, and already have quotes and specified service proposals.

At this stage, you don't need to pay any solicitor deposits yet. Just confirm with the solicitor that you would like to go forward with them, and ideally already firm up whom you will be working with. When you make an offer and suddenly have it accepted, the agent will ask you about your solicitor. If you have all this lined up, you simply say 'go' to the solicitor, pay the few hundred Pounds deposit, and off you go. If you need to research solicitors when you had an offer accepted, it might become quite stressful and you will feel time pressure, as the house may stay on the market until a solicitor is instructed.

Chapter 6

Viewing and offering

6. VIEWING AND OFFERING

After all this preparation and theory, now we are starting to get hands on with your property purchase. In this chapter, we'll go through the viewing and offering stage. You might repeat this a couple of times – particularly, expect to view quite a few properties – before you agree on a purchase. That is fine. Here, we take a look at things that will hopefully make the process a little easier for you:

- Viewings and how to book and prepare for them.

- Questions you may want to ask the agent.

- Preparing the offer, including what different pricings mean, competition and what to write.

- Negotiation – don't expect your first offer to be accepted.

- Offer acceptance.

Chapter 6 contents

6.1 Viewings

Before you go

As described in Chapter 4.2, you can do a certain amount of exploration before you go for the viewing on Google maps using the satellite feature and – actually – also the street view feature:

https://www.google.com/maps

Have a look whether there are any no-goes. For example, you might not want to live next to a landfill or close to a school that will block off traffic every morning. By doing these basic checks, you make sure that you don't waste time going to a property where you can already tell from a distance that you won't buy it.

When you start with the house hunt, the first few properties may feel very confusing: you have no idea whether the size is normal, state of repair is normal and what it is that really attracts you. Hence, it will be wise to do a few viewing to just get a feel for the local housing market. After seeing 10 urban semis, you might come to realise that other than the kitchen extension or conservatory, they are all the same size and there is nothing bigger to be found by viewing 10 more. After seeing 5 homes at the bottom of the market range, you might come to realise that you will be guaranteed to get mouldy old windows, knackered interior and astonishing electrics. Get a feel for what really puts you off and what you can live with and fix, so that you don't miss out on your potentially perfect long-term home due to initial shock value.

Booking a viewing

Once you have found a few properties which you like the look of, the next step is to view them. Depending on the route the vendor took to put them on the market, you either book the viewing through the agent or through an online form (e.g. for Purplebricks). If you book through an agent, always call them – don't expect them to get back to a query submitted online. Especially if the house has a decent amount of interest, they might never go through the effort of contacting you back.

You should usually have a choice of days and times when you can view the property. The basic decision is: weekday or weekend. If you pick a weekend viewing, expect to share the slot with another five, ten or twenty interested buyers, and this can be very awkward and uncomfortable. Open Houses at weekends may feel like a pub on a Friday night. If you pick a weekday slot during working hours, chances are you'll be the only one looking at the property. That gives you more time with the agent and doesn't create a sense of competition. If there are a few properties you like the look of, consider taking a day off work to view all of them for direct comparison. If you are the only one there, the agent will also have a lot more time for you and you have the opportunity to befriend your agent, which will help you in the long run.

Always be friendly and polite, no matter how frantic a viewing is. If you are competing with 10 other buyers, you don't want the agent to remember you as a twat. This is easier said than done though if the agent stands around playing with his phone and doesn't give you any answers. Try to focus on what you are trying to achieve.

Preparation and what to look for

When you go for a viewing, make sure you are prepared: have the basic facts about the house to hand, have a list of questions, make a plan what you want to inspect. 'Which' actually offers a nifty little check-list which you can take with you:

https://static.money.product.which.co.uk/money/media/documents/5a b8a9a66649b-house-viewing-checklist-460398.pdf

You can add to this further points that are important.

When you view the property, remember to look past decoration and examine the stuff that will cost a lot to fix. This includes:

- Cracks in the outside render and/or brickwork.

- Damage to external features.

- Missing or broken tiles on the roof and evidence of the roof having been replaced at some point.

- Evidence of leaks in the loft.

- State of the guttering and evidence of external leaks.

- Windows:

    o Evidence of internal condensation?

    o Double glazing?

    o Do the seals still work?

    o Do they open and close fine?

- Damp to the inside walls (feel and look for mould).

- Tap around the window frames and parts of walls – is it hollow?

- How old and in what state is the electrical consumer unit and electrical wiring?

- How old and in what state is the boiler?

- Does it smell damp or mouldy?

You can then go ahead and test a few basic things by turning them on (yes, you can do that):

- Tap and shower water pressure and hot water.

- Lights.

- Hob/oven.

- Open the doors to all fitted units that you will inherit.

Finally, the house itself is not everything. We have seen properties where the neighbour had erected a fully functioning radio station including all transmission with a 4-meter antenna. So have a look around the property and out of the windows and check for example for the following:

- How tidy do the neighbours look and what is the state of repairs of their property? If they get a leak or their roof falls apart, you will also have problems.

- What is the situation with offspring? Are there kids, and if so, are they nice or are they doing drive-bys on mopeds?

- Is there a street light right in front of your window or property? That will illuminate your room at night and also might make putting in a driveway impossible.

- Is the property surrounded by huge trees, and if so, are they within your boundary? Big trees might throw your garden into shade for most of the day. In worst case, they might fall over in a storm if they are unfit. If they belong to neighbours, you most likely can't do anything about it. If they are in your garden, you'd have to pay someone for knocking them down or trimming them (unless you are good with that). Attention here: if trees have a tree preservation order on them, you can't touch them. Check this with the agent before committing. Your solicitor will later on also be able to check, but by that time you're already at least a few hundred Pounds down.

- Have any of the neighbours done any extension work that you could mirror? Having precedents around is a good thing if you are planning to extend the property.

Also, take a note of everything the vendor might have changed – knocked out walls, extended kitchens etc. You can then follow up with the agent about these to find out when and by whom they were done and whether they were certified or may turn out a DIY project gone wrong. As usual, get everything in writing if it is important.

Second viewing

Remember, if you like it, go back a second time at a different time of day. Memory is a funny thing, and that way you can look at the property with fresh eyes and without the rose-tinted spectacles of the first viewing when everything was a first impression. This also shows to agent and vendor that you are truly interested. Don't leave too much time between the two viewings if the property receives a lot of interest. You can also put your starting offer in and then come back for a second viewing before continuing the negotiation.

Potential pitfalls for later repairs and expenses

When viewing the property, it will be most helpful if you look for vendor lifestyle choices that would give you a lot more work than you are bargaining for. As a rule of thumb, see how these people live, how much attention to detail they display and whether they seem to have cared about the property.

- Is the vendor a smoker? It will be hard or impossible to get the smell out without massive investment and/or DIY effort. You'd have to rip out all carpets, wallpapers and anything else that took on the smell.

- Does the vendor have a dog? Most people who bought from vendors with a dog subsequently found that they had to re-carpet because of pee puddles (old or new) and the related smell and stain. As unlikely it may sound while the dog is hidden away or looking cute, if you buy from vendors with a dog, plan for this and the associated cost and time.

- Does the vendor have a cat? Cat allergens will be everywhere. You might have to get rid of all soft furnishings if you have a cat allergy.

- Has the vendor maintained the property well? Look for bad paint jobs, broken tiles, poor plastering etc. If there is evidence that they have done some bodged DIY where you can spot it, chances are high that you will find a lot more trouble once the property is yours.

- Has the vendor used reputable companies or mates to carry out works? Again, you might get more than you are asking for if you buy a house full of undocumented installations that fell off a truck somewhere.

- Is the house humid, smelly, dirty or otherwise uncomfortable to be in? The vendors should have dressed the property up as good as they can to sell it to you. If even then it doesn't measure up, it won't magically get better after you offered on it.

In summary: use your senses and trust your instinct. If the house smells mouldy, it is mouldy. If it smells damp, it is damp. If you can hear neighbours screaming through the walls, you have bad neighbours. If there are 5 dogs barking in the gardens around you, they will still be there when you move in. If there is a decomposing car in the back garden, it might still be there later. The estate agent will say anything to make you feel differently. Don't listen – it is you who will have to fix the mess later on, while no-one else will care about it. Of course – if you are happy to take this on, go for it.

6.2 Questions for the agent

6.2.1 Questions which you can expect answers for

Once you are at the viewing, you can ask the agent any question you want. Lots of insightful things have been written about all that you should ask, and you should. However, what no-one writes about is that you typically won't get an answer. At the viewing, expect the agent to answer pretty much every question with:

- "I don't know, but I can find out for you".

Alternatively, they may answer with:

- "I don't know, but it looks fine".

- "I don't know, but this is no different from all houses of this era".

- "I don't know, but I can't see any work that needs doing in this house".

What are you supposed to do with that? Well, you are supposed to shut up and buy the thing. But that's not good enough. So, go with the first option – ask them to find out for you. Ideally, get them to send you answers in writing.

There are a lot of things you can ask. Amongst the ones we found most useful are the following:

- Has the vendor carried out any works? If yes, what and when?
- How old are
    - Boiler
    - Heating system
    - Electrics
    - Roof
    - Windows
- Has any part of the house ever been altered (extensions, wall removals etc.)?
- Why is the vendor moving and what is their timeline?
- Is the property in a chain and has the vendor found an onward purchase or are they still looking? If so, what is their timeline?
- How long have the vendors lived there?
- Have offers been made on the property and/or has anyone offered asking price? What is the interest like?
- What is included with the sale?
- Can you speak directly to the sellers?
- How does this property compare to property xyz which you viewed with them?

Also, ask about any observations you might make during viewing that raise your eyebrows.

Be aware that any answers you get might be wrong, especially if not in writing. Agents show a lot of properties and do get things mixed up. If there is an important point which you base your decision to buy on, check and check again, ideally both talking to the owner and agent and having confirmation in writing.

6.2.2 Questions which you can't expect answers for (try anyway if you want)

There is a lot of guidance out there suggesting a lot of smart things that you can ask the agent. From experience, here is a list of questions you are unlikely to get a (useful/truthful) answer for:

- What is the local area like?

- What is the minimum price the seller will accept?

- Have there been any problems with the boiler recently?

- Does the area have any hidden issues to be aware of?

- Who are the neighbours and what are they like?

- Are there good local amenities?

- Is there room for negotiation? – You don't ask that, you'll try and soon find out

You can, however, have more luck if you ask the vendor directly while viewing.

6.3 Buying a property in need of work

If you are inclined to do some work, or even if your agent was good with his/her photographic angles that make a skip look like a palace, you will come across properties in various states of 'trashed'. This may range from a 'grandma' home that belonged to an old person and was looked after well but never renewed, to a property smashed to bits by drunk students. When making a decision about a property that requires repairs, the guiding principle No #1 should be structural soundness: no matter how bad things look, there should be no danger of the thing falling apart. If the property is structurally sound (and you likely need a surveyor to check that), you will then assess how much repairing it will cost you and how long it will take. The table below gives a rough guidance as to how much different aspects of a 'project' may cost.

Table 20. Approximate cost of fixing a project house. Depending on how much DIY you want to do, you might bring some of these costs down a lot. Also, see whether a builder gives you a good quote for doing everything as a package.

Work	Duration	Approximate Cost
Full roof replacement (new roof tiles)	1 month	£10,000 – £20,000
Re-laying the roof (recycling tiles)	2 weeks	£5,000 - £10,000
Gas central heating incl. boiler and all radiators and pipe work	2 weeks	£3,000 - £4,000
New boiler only	1 day	£1,500 - £3,000
Full electrical rewire	1 week	£3,000
Full kitchen installation	2 weeks	£3,000 - £5,000
Full bathroom installation	2 weeks	£3,000 – 5,000
Replacement of all windows	1 week	£5,000 - £10,000
Full carpeting	1 week	£2,000 - £4,000
Full re-decoration	2 weeks	£2,000 - £5,000

6.4 Preparation of the offer

If you are happy with the viewing(s) and would like to buy the property, you have to put in an offer. Usually, can email this offer across; make sure you write that you are offering 'subject to contract', which means that the price can be negotiated if e.g. the survey brings up costly problems. The government has the following to say about making offers:

- A buyer must make an offer through the estate agent if a home is sold through one.

- A buyer can make their offer directly to the seller for a private sale.

- Buyers can make offers verbally (over the phone or in person) or in writing.

- An offer isn't legally binding in England and Wales until contracts are exchanged.

- If a buyer makes an offer 'subject to contract', this means the price can still be negotiated (e.g. if a survey finds a problem with the property).

Source: *https://www.gov.uk/buy-sell-your-home/offers*

You can also explicitly make you offer subject to contract and survey – not everyone might be aware that subject to contract implies a satisfactory survey.

An agent has the obligation to bring any offer forward to the vendor, so you should expect that. An agent may say that the vendor won't accept you offer anyway; push them to bring it forward despite that to get the ball rolling. Remember to be friendly.

6.4.1 How much?

How much you offer depends on for example:

- How long the property has been on the market.

- How many people you are competing with / the interest in the property.

- The phrasing of the price – check which price category (below) the vendor chose.

Price categories

Here are the typical price 'categories' that you have to look out for:

- Just the price: "£250,000". You can offer less, and are expected to do so unless there is lots of competition.

- "Offers in region of (**O.I.R.O**) £250,000". The vendor is expecting to get less. Offer less.

- "Offers in excess of (**O.I.E.O**) £250,000". The vendor expects £250,000 to be the absolute minimum price. Expect to offer more, especially if there is competition. If there is no interest, you can still offer less and see what comes back.

- "**Guide price** £250,000". This is a weird one. It seems to come from auctions. From what we have seen, this price is typically below market value to attract interest, and you can expect it to go for (a lot) more once people start a bidding war. We viewed one house that had a guide price on Purplebricks of £170,000, received 15 offers and sold somewhere around £190,000. It wasn't worth it. You are being fooled through a bidding war.

When you make your first offer, unless there is good reason to offer the asking price, always offer below. You will be expected to negotiate, and the only way is up. If there is good reason to believe that the house won't fly off the shelf and you have room to negotiate, a good way to start is to offer in region of 10% below the asking price. You can try less than that (especially if there are big repairs), but if you are too frivolous, you won't get anywhere, you'll just get a 'no' rather than a negotiation. If the property is on the market for 'offers in excess off', you could try a little under the asking price first – you might get a yes if they have not much interest.

6.4.2 Competition and times

Be aware that the agent will use your offer to drum up more/better ones. While your offer cannot be disclosed, once an agent has any kind of offer, they may happily tell you that:

a) "We already have an offer on this property" (likely: less than asking price).

b) "Someone already offered asking price" (ditto).

c) "Someone already offered more than the asking price" (ditto).

In theory, agents are not allowed to lie and this should give you an indication of your competition. Also be aware that if you put in an offer early on, expect the agent to fish around for better offers for a few days. If you don't like that, you can try to come to an agreement quickly by making your offer valid for 24 hours. It's a gamble, like so many other things. However, don't let the agent drag you along for weeks; if after a week you still don't have an answer despite negotiations, chances are you are just being used to push someone else up. Be prepared to walk away and withdraw your offer. That might also finally get their attention.

One of the worst things that can happen to you is competing with an investor or builder/property developer. The former will do minimum work to the property and just rent it out to milk it and in the future cash in on a much higher price. So they are prepared to pay above the odds, because they won't fix it anyway. The latter can do most works themselves at a cost much lower than what it would cost you. If you are competing with either of those, expect the property to sell above the odds – both parties can afford to pay more, as long-term they will make the money back. In this case, you have to decide whether you want to pay more, or whether you walk away. This might even mean that some areas which are 'hot' for investors become too expensive for you to buy, given what you get for the money.

6.4.3 Offer in writing

When you prepare your offer, remember your pitch from the previous section, and merge it in. For example, you can write:

> *"Thank you for your time showing us around 45 York Street on Thursday. We really like the house and decided to put in an offer of £160,000 subject to contract and survey. We appreciate this is below the advertised price, but we are aware that the house needs replacement of all windows and substantial work to the roof. Our offer reflects the anticipated costs for these works.*
>
> *We have an Agreement in Principle for our mortgage and saved up a sufficient deposit. We have no chain, currently living in rented accommodation with a 1-month notice period. We are a couple looking to move to Darvesley to live closer to work and friends and settle down. Andy is a full-time regulatory lead at a chemical plant. Laura is a full-time lecturer at university. We are first time buyers and are looking forward to hearing from you."*

Expect to hear back fairly quickly, i.e. same or next day.

6.5 Negotiation

Many people feel that this is hard; you have to haggle! But give it a go. There are a lot of strategies to negotiation. In the end, you have to do something that you feel comfortable with. As some basic advice, before going into the negotiation, work out for yourself the following points:

- What is your **position**? This is what you say to the agent in terms of what you want. This is driven by the two points below:

o   What are your **needs**? This is what you absolutely have to achieve; e.g. you might be unable to spend more than £180,000. You don't tell the agent that. But this is where you draw the line to walk away; if you keep being pushed up, this would be your 'best and final offer'.

o   What are your **wants**? This is what you would like to happen. This could for example be the price you would like to pay in an ideal scenario. That's what you tell the agent and if you get it as the outcome, you should feel happy that you got a deal you consider decent.

In a negotiation, always start lower than your 'perfect' price. So if you'd like to pay around £180,000 to £184,000 for a house that is on the market at £190,000, make your first offer something like £170,000. They'll most likely turn you down. Then offer £175,000. If they turn you down again, say let's meet in the middle at £182,000. If they still don't take it, go in much smaller increments or walk away. If you start the negotiation at £182,000, you don't have anywhere to go – you'd be expected to go up to £186,000 or more, most commonly, unless the vendor is desperate to sell. And the vendor will most likely expect you to go up on your initial offer unless there is no interest or you offer the asking price– that's just psychological. It shows that you are prepared to make concessions, too.

The negotiation process may feel alien to you. It might be cheeky, but it can then be good to put in a 'practice' offer on a property that you don't like so much, just to get the hang of the process. Go in low and then work your way through the negotiation. In the end you can always walk away – an offer is not binding. After all, you don't want to screw up your first ever negotiation if it is the house you really want: get some practice first! At the same time, don't upset an agent that you later need to buy from.

The negotiation is often better done over the phone. You get more context as to what the vendor is thinking, and it doesn't come across as if you are an evil robot. Always explain your position and why you are limited in what you can pay.

6.6 Offer acceptance and what is next

If the negotiation is successful, your offer will be accepted. Typically, the agent calls you up with the good news. FIRST CELEBRATION! This marks the start to a couple of very stressful months, so have a beer or something.

The next chapter will go through the things that should follow immediately after offer acceptance to make sure you don't lose your treasure.

6.7 Further info

- The UK government actually has advice on the process here:

  https://www.gov.uk/buy-sell-your-home/offers

- Rightmove has helpful guidance on the offer process here:

  https://www.rightmove.co.uk/advice/buyer/buying-a-property/making-an-offer/

Chapter 7

Offer accepted: preparing the next steps

7. OFFER ACCEPTED: PREPARING THE NEXT STEPS

In this chapter, we have a look at what comes next once your offer has been accepted. If you have not yet planned ahead beyond viewings, the speed and amount of decisions you have to make might catch you by surprise. Here, we take a look at things that happen immediately after offer acceptance (on the same day or within a few days, unless you want to run into delays):

- Paperwork to be completed with the agent; often, this is required to take your property off the market.

- Instructing your solicitor and first steps in working with your solicitor.

- Planning the survey with your surveyor.

- Getting your full mortgage offer.

- Sketching out initial timelines with your agent and solicitor.

Chapter 7 contents

7.1 Agent paperwork

Once you had the good news that your offer was accepted, what should happen immediately next is the following. Don't wait, as most commonly your property will hang around on the market until you complete these steps.

7.1.1 Visit the agent to show evidence of ID and funds

Remember the chapter on getting your stuff ready? Now you are laughing. You can get this done the same day. The agent does several checks to verify that you are actually able to afford the house and that you are not lying. While this goes on, the property will usually remain for sale. Hence, get it done ASAP.

Present the evidence

You will have to go to the agent to show proof of

- ID
- Address
- Deposit (bank statements)
- Employment / wages (payslips)
- Agreement in principle

Possibly the agent may request further items; check with them.

Instruct your solicitor

Often, the agent will expect you to give details of your solicitor before taking the property off the market. Remember the chapter on finding and lining up a solicitor? If you already chose one, you can do this very quickly. All the agent typically needs is the name/contact details and address.

7.1.2 Agent takes the property off the market

Once it is verified that you are a legitimate buyer, your agent should take the property off the market immediately. Ask for them to do so, and check that they do so. The listing should now show as "Sold STC". This means sold, subject to contract. It basically indicates that the property is gone, unless either of you pulls out of the sale before exchanging contracts or completion.

Once you got to this milestone, you can breathe for a moment. No-one else should be able to snatch the home from you and the proper buying process has begun. Gazumping is seemingly not legal anymore, i.e. the agent is not allowed to sell the home to a higher bidder after it is off the market. The only thing that could happen is that the vendor changes their mind, and you are not in control of that.

7.2 Instruct your solicitor

When you instruct your solicitor to handle the purchase, you are typically expected to meet in person and bring a range of paperwork. To get the ball rolling, you will be expected to pay a solicitor deposit in the range of £300. You then have to make sure that your solicitor actually does get started – once they got their deposit and don't have to tout for your business anymore, they might suddenly be a lot less active.

7.2.1 Paperwork required to get started

When you go to see the solicitor, you are typically expected to have the following items to hand:

- Proof of ID

- Proof of address

- Evidence of funds

- Possible Agreement in Principle for the mortgage

You will also be expected to read and sign paperwork and provide information, including

- Terms and Conditions of the solicitor

- Initial Instruction Form

- Stamp Duty Form

- Money Laundering Declarations

- Joint ownership / shared ownership form

- Gifted deposit (if someone gifts you a deposit, consult with a solicitor as early as possible)

The solicitor should send you these forms in advance. Ask for a list of exact items to bring to the appointment.

When you formalise working with your solicitor, make sure that you receive the following in writing:

- Name and status of the person carrying out the conveyancing

- Name of that person's supervisor

- Complaints procedure

Buying together: joint tenants vs. tenants in common

If you buy together, you have to decide which of these two options you want to go for:

Joint tenants means that if the person you are buying with dies, his/her part of the property is automatically transferred over to you. Otherwise, both parties own half of the property.

Tenants in common means that each person buying the house will have a specific share of the property attributed to his/her name. In case of death, this is transferred to his/her estate, not necessarily the other partner buying the property. If you want to make sure that your share of the property goes to the person you are buying with, you might need an additional will if you choose tenants in common.

7.2.2 Connecting up your solicitor to agent and mortgage lender

Your solicitor will require details of your Mortgage Lender (if any) and of your Estate Agent. Make sure you provide as much detail as possible for the Estate Agent, including

- The name of the contact person handling your property sale

- Phone number and email address

- The full office address

- The name of the estate agency

Being precise and detailed will minimise the risk of information being sent to the wrong person or branch and your process already starting with delays as everyone waits for the impossible.

It is actually a good thing to check with your agent whether your solicitor has made contact. If the agent has not heard from the solicitor, they can chase it up. Make sure you also give your agent precise details for your solicitor, including name, phone number and email address.

Finally, make sure that your solicitor receives the **memo of sale**, respectively the **confirmation of sale** from the agent. If they don't receive this, they may just sit and wait, not doing anything. Check with both, agent and solicitor, that this has been sent and received.

7.3 Arranging the survey

7.3.1 The standard procedure

While your solicitor gets started, you should next plan on when you'd like to have the survey carried out, unless you feel you don't need a survey. Typically, survey and conveyancing are started at the same time, since the survey results will inform the solicitor.

Most surveyors will have lead times – the waiting time between you asking them to do the survey and them actually being able to do so. Make sure you double-check this with your surveyor now, so that you can plan ahead. If you have a nice surveyor, they will book you in say 3 weeks in advance but give you flexibility to reschedule should something happen down the line. Ask your surveyor whether they do that.

7.3.2 What if you are in a chain?

If you are in a chain, make sure you don't blow your money on survey and conveyancing too early. If you know that your vendor still needs to find an onward purchase, you can ask your solicitor to wait with searches and other activities until the vendor found somewhere and started their own process. Similarly, there is no point carrying out the survey too early. Remember your vendor will go through the same process as you, so even if you start a month in advance, they will still have to catch up. You won't buy much time, but may lose the money you paid for activities if your vendor for example can't find a new home and pulls out. You can discuss strategy with your solicitor.

7.4 Mortgage offer

Now it's time to turn your agreement in principle into a real mortgage offer. Scoop up all the documents you prepared (payslips, proof of deposit etc) and book a mortgage appointment. You may have to wait a few days for an appointment to become available. Allow 2 to 3 hours for the appointment – you'll go through many questions and guidance, and the time is worth it. At the mortgage appointment, you will have to make the following decisions, amongst others:

- Amount of the mortgage.

- Mortgage term.

- Tracker of fixed rate.

- Period for which the rate is guaranteed.

- Upfront fee or not.

Further, you will most likely run through a whole medical questionnaire in order to get you an initial quote for **life and critical illness cover**.

Following the mortgage appointment, your lender will send someone out to value your property. A few days to a week or more after this was done, the bank will issue the mortgage offer, unless they think the house is not worth the amount of money you offered.

Assume the time from appointment to receipt of the mortgage offer to take around 2-3 weeks. The earlier you do it, the easier you can curb your losses should the lender decide not to offer you a mortgage for the property.

7.5 Sketching out timelines

In the beginning, you will find that no-one wants to commit to any timelines. Try to get as much in writing and agreed as you can – find out when vendors want to move, what the bottlenecks are etc. This is important so you can plan your holidays around the process, plan when to roughly move and get out of your rental contract, start of any works etc. In the beginning, this might be accurate to a month or two or even more. However, at least it gets you (and everyone else) in the right mindset. We have heard of houses that after one year had still not changed hands because the owner could not find something new that he liked. That is just not acceptable. As usual, don't expect your solicitor to commit to anything, and make sure you send instructions regarding timelines in writing. If they don't do anything for a month, you can complain if they know that you are expecting to complete.

The point at which timelines will be firmed up and decided is exchange of contract. At this point, everyone will commit to a moving date, and there will be penalties for either party to screw those up.

Chapter 8

Conveyancing from start to finish

8. CONVEYANCING FROM START TO FINISH

We are now leaving the realm of excitement and dive into conveyancing, the legal process of buying the home that you had your offer accepted on. Brace yourself, this time period will most likely massively suck and stress you out. Remember that almost everyone goes through the same, and that you too will make it to the end eventually.

The basic role of the conveyancing process is for your solicitor / conveyancer to do legal due diligence on your home through searches and enquiries, manage Land Registry entries, draw up contracts, handle stamp duty and exchange of cash as well as providing legal advice to you. In parallel, you will carry out your own checks through survey, follow-on checks and potentially quotes for repairs. In this Chapter, we hence run through the following in detail so that you can develop a better understanding of what is supposed to happen:

- The conveyancing process dismantled, looking at guidelines what the solicitor should be doing, documents you can expect to receive as part of the contract pack, searches, raising queries, re-negotiation, provisional contract signing, 10% deposit, bank transfers and communication.

- The survey: planning ahead, what you can expect from a full survey report and acting on your survey report.

- Other checks that may become necessary, such as inspection of electrics or damp.

- Getting quotes for required works.

- Tips for staying on top of everything.

We then look at exchange of contracts and completion, which is the first point where you enter a binding agreement to buy the property. At **exchange of contracts**, you will put down a deposit typically amounting to 10% of the purchase price, and you'll lose that if you pull out, plus you may be made to pay compensation. Exchange of contracts is followed by **completion**, which is when you get the keys. These activities go hand in hand with actions your solicitor has to conduct, such as paying stamp duty, registering you with the Land Registry and handling your mortgage. It is important to be very diligent during this time, as any mistakes may cause delays and cost a lot.

Chapter 8 contents

8.1 The conveyancing process

Before we get into this, let's have a look at the conveyancing timeline from offer acceptance to you getting the keys. The following sections will go through all of the associated steps in detail.

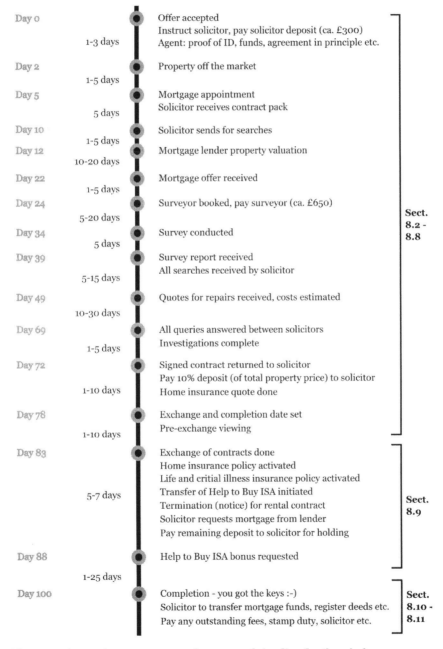

Figure 24. Approximate sequence of events and timeline for the whole conveyancing process. This may take less or more time depending on your circumstances.

8.2 Start to pre-exchange: what should the solicitor be doing?

This has been one of the hardest things to figure out, until... I found the Law Society's Conveyancing Protocol! You can download it here:

https://www.lawsociety.org.uk/support-services/advice/articles/conveyancing-protocol/

The summary below will take you through the most important actions which your surveyor should be conducting when acting on behalf of the buyer (that is: you!). Is your solicitor not doing anything? Are you missing information? Here is the stick to poke them with! Now you got ammunition to ask, because you know what is supposed to happen. It's a goldmine!

Stage A: Instructions

We halve already covered the beginning of instructing your solicitor in Section 7.2 after having your offer accepted. Once you got the ball rolling by telling the solicitor that you had the offer accepted and want to get going, the solicitor should also inform you of the following:

- Advise you to get quotes for building insurance in keeping with your mortgage provider's requirements.

- Check whether the seller is entitled to sell and/or whether power of attorney may be required (if you buy in a scenario where e.g. an old lady is in a care home and her children sell her house to fund this).

- Give you an update on cost estimates compared to your initial quotation.

- Advise you with regards to "any dependent purchase or sale": this would be relevant if you are in a chain, for example.

Stage B: Pre-exchange – submitting a contract

Within five days of the solicitor receiving the confirmation of sale (respectively memo of sale) from the agent, the activities below should commence. You should expect your solicitor to explain delays beyond the five days to yourself and the vendor's solicitor. Your solicitor should now do the following:

Contract Bundle

- Confirm your instructions, remind you of your stamp duty liability and recommend carrying out your own survey.

- Check identity of the vendor's solicitor, follow SRA and Law Society standards, file all information related to your sale; confirm instructions with vendor's solicitor, and coordinate related sales; confirm the use of the Law Society's Protocol.

- Potentially talk through your funding arrangements.

- Confirm the vendor's timescales, also for all related transactions.

- Provide you with obtained information regarding the chain and related purchases by the vendor.

- Confirm receipt of the contract bundle from the vendor's solicitor with you. You should receive a copy of this.

Searches

- Request searches as soon as possible, unless instructed to wait.

- Manage need for planning permissions.

- Raise queries with the vendor's solicitor arising from.

  o Your solicitor's assessment of information received

  o Your own questions

  o Please note that your solicitor is advised to not raise queries which can be answered through the obtained information already

- Send you a copy of the received documentation and the results of investigations. This should occur as an ongoing process – your solicitor should NOT wait for all information to come back before passing it on to you.

Other items

- Discuss the impact of apportionments of the purchase price with you.

- Confirm and check the mortgage offer with you and the mortgage lender.

- Discuss joint/shared ownership with you.

- Manage contract amendments.

End of phase

- Approve and return to the vendor's solicitor the following:

    ○ Draft contract provisions.

    ○ Transfer, if any.

Stage C: Prior to exchange of contracts

Progressing to exchange of contracts

- Send you the contract for signature.

- Explain your obligations regarding:

    ○ Insurance.

    ○ Deposit (not the final one for the mortgage, but usually a 10% deposit of the purchase price required at exchange of contracts).

- Ask you to transfer the deposit (again, not the one for the mortgage, but the pre-exchange deposit). Remember, transferring large sums of money can take several days to a week, so plan for this early.

    ○ **WARNING**: there is now a popular scam that has seen buyers lose their deposit. It is called **'Friday afternoon fraud'**. What basically happens is that fraudsters intercept the solicitor's and/or your email chain. They will then email you – from the exact solicitor's email address! – that you should transfer funds to an alternative account. NEVER EVER ACT ON SUCH INSTRUCTIONS. Only transfer money to the account which you have in writing on a document directly from the solicitor, such as on your quote. Prior to transfer, you can also call your solicitor (using their official number, not that from a potential spoof mail) and ask whether bank details are correct. If you send money to a fraudster account, you might not get it back. It is called Friday afternoon fraud because that's when many transactions happen and it gives fraudsters most time to 'get away with it' over the weekend. You cannot be careful enough here.

- Prepare for signatures of stamp duty and mortgage and prepare the stamp duty return.

- If you are in a chain, provide the fullest information possible regarding the status of other transactions in your chain.

- Confirm the completion date with you and the vendor in consideration of and communication with all other parties in the chain. Request your solicitor or the agent to agree a date if necessary.

- Advise you regarding the funds you have to have ready.

- Remind you of the required building insurance, which has to be in place either from date of completion or from date of exchange; your solicitor should tell you which of the two is applicable.

Acting on behalf of the lender

- Check whether there are conditions in the mortgage offer that need to be satisfied, and act on them.

In the following sections (Section 8.3 to 8.8), we will look at the above lists and items in more detail.

8.3 Activities and items from your solicitor up to pre-exchange

8.3.1 Contract Pack / Contract Bundle

The first thing that your solicitor should receive is the 'contract pack' or 'contract bundle'. This should then be passed on to you by your solicitor. The contract pack should include the following, and may contain further items:

- The draft contract with 'Standard Conditions of Sale'

- A copy of Register of Title and Title Plan (dated recently)

  - If applicable, also a copy of the registered lease

- o If applicable, an explanation of the seller's title if the name of the registered owner is different from the seller; in this case, your solicitor may also need to initiate rectifying the register

- A pre-drafted Land Registry TR1 form

- The Law Society's Property Information Form (TA6)

- The Law Society's Fittings and Contents Form (TA10)

- For *new builds*: New Home Information form (TA8)

- Planning permission and/or building regulation approval and certification for any alterations or additions to the property

- Required consents where applicable

- Searches and enquiries made on behalf of the seller

- The Energy Performance Certificate (EPC); you might already have this from the agent

The information contained within the above documents marks the starting point for the due diligence process. In theory, your solicitor should deal with it adequately and raise all issues that are apparent. In practice, you better make sure that you read through everything in detail and flag all unknowns and open question with the solicitor ASAP.

When you receive the initial information, you should make sure that all claims match up with what you saw at the property. Remember, your solicitor never saw the place and doesn't know whether the vendors have a bunch of trees in the garden or not.

Register of Title and Title Plan

These documents prove that the seller owns the property and has the right to sell it. They will also show exemptions from ownership. Both are obtained by the solicitor from HM Land Registry at around £3 each.

The **Register of Title** contains the following sections:

- A: Property Register. This describes the land and estate which is included in the title.

- B: Proprietorship Register. This identifies the title class and owner and also includes entries that affect selling the property.

- C: Charges Register. This specifies any charges affecting the land.

You can look at an example here:

https://eservices.landregistry.gov.uk/eservices/FindAProperty/view/res
ources/example_register.pdf

Your solicitor should check that there is nothing adversarial in the Register of Title. Read through it yourself and pass any questions about it on to your solicitor in writing.

The **Title Plan** indicates which bit of land you are buying. It shows:

- Title number of the land

- The land included in the title, typically edged in red

It looks something like this:

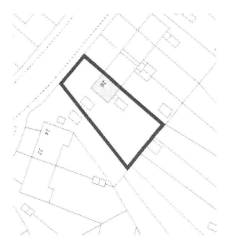

Figure 25. Example of the highlighted piece of land that you should find on your title plan.

You can look at a full example here:

https://eservices.landregistry.gov.uk/eservices/FindAProperty/view/res
ources/example_title_plan.pdf

You should check that the drawn boundaries match what you think you are buying and let your solicitor know if there are any discrepancies.

You can also have a look whether any extensions or permanent structures are part of this drawing. If not, query it with your solicitor to see whether they would need building regulatory approval.

Land registry TR1 form

This is the draft for the transfer of title deeds. Make sure you check it ten times – all names have to be spelled correctly etc. You can find the template for this form here:

https://www.gov.uk/government/publications/registered-titles-whole-transfer-tr1

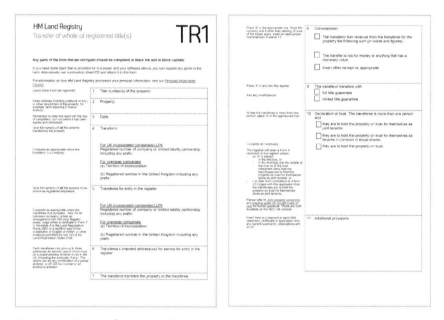

Figure 26. HM Land Registry TR1 form example, page 1 and 2 out of 3 total pages (as of May 2018). ©HM Land Registry/gov.uk

The Law Society's Property Information Form (TA6)

This is a pre-defined legal document that has the purpose of catching issues associated with the property early. It is to be filled in by the vendor. You need to check whether all information provided is accurate and correct. Ask your solicitor about anything you are not sure about. Your solicitor should check whether any issues are apparent from the information given and raise enquiries with the vendor's solicitor accordingly. You can download an example here:

https://www.lawsociety.org.uk/support-services/documents/TA6-form-specimen

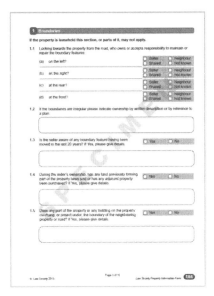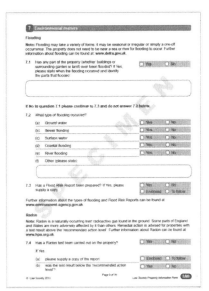

Figure 27. The Law Society's TA6 form (specimen), two random pages. ©Law Society

The form provides information on the following aspects of the property and land:

- Boundaries
- Disputes and complaints
- Notices and proposals
- Alterations, planning and building control
- Guarantees and warranties
- Insurance
- Environmental matters
- Rights and informal arrangements
- Parking
- Other charges
- Occupiers
- Services
- Connection to utilities and services
- Transaction information

Law Society's Fixture and Fittings form (TA10)

This is a pre-defined legal document that has the purpose of making explicitly clear what is staying at the property and what is going. For each item, it will detail whether it is included, excluded or whether there is none. Again, check this carefully and raise any questions with your solicitor. When you move in and the boiler has disappeared, this is the document you need to demonstrate that the boiler should in fact be there.

You can download an example here:

https://www.lawsociety.org.uk/support-services/documents/TA10-form-specimen/

Figure 28. The Law Society's TA10 form (specimen), two random pages. ©Law Society

The form provides information on the following areas of the house and what you can expect to find there:

- Basic fittings

- Kitchen

- Bathroom

- Carpets

- Curtains and curtain rails

- Light fittings

- Fitted units

- Outdoor area

- TV and telephone

- Stock of fuel

- Other items

For new builds: New Home Information form (TA8)

If you are buying a new build, then you should receive information on it as soon as possible. Make sure your receive a TA8; you can download and example here:

https://www.lawsociety.org.uk/support-services/documents/TA8-form-specimen/

8.3.2 Searches

After checking through the basic information shared about the house in the forms filled in by the vendors, your solicitor will 'send for searches'. Basically, in most cases this means that your solicitor will use a sub-contractor to carry out searcher on their behalf. These searches are there to retrieve information about the property from the council. Searches may take some time to come back, from a week to a month or more, depending how busy the council is. Let's go through the list of the most common searches:

Local search

Cost: around £60 to £400 depending on the local authority.

Duration: around 1 to 6 weeks depending on the local authority and time of the year.

The local search gets information on everything that the council 'inflicts' on your property and gives context what situation you are buying into. This search may include information on:

- Local land charge entries

- Planning history

- Building regulations applications
- Planning designations and proposals
- Roads
- Public rights of way
- Other matters
- Road schemes
- Rail
- Schemes, notices and orders
- Community infrastructure levy
- Contaminated land
- Radon gas
- Assets of community value
- Green deal and coal checker

It is important that your solicitor reads through the outcome in detail, as they should spot things that you don't even know how to look for. Your solicitor should then send a summary of the report to you highlighting

- What is unusual
- What you should think about or follow up
- What will impact on your life at the property
- What is 'normal' and why

If your solicitor just forwards the results without comment, consider asking for answers to these basic questions.

Water and Drainage search

Cost: around £50 to £80 depending on the local authority.

Duration: around 1 to 3 weeks depending on the local authority and time of the year.

The water and drainage search reveals where the water and drainage pipe work runs relative to your property. This matters, as there will be restrictions on building close to it. If for example you want a shed at the end of the garden but the council has a water main running down there, you might not be able to go ahead.

The water and drainage search will include information on the following:

- Maps showing nearest public sewer and water pipes
- Whether foul drainage from the property drains to a public sewer
- Whether surface water from the property drains to a public sewer
- Any adoption agreements for sewers
- Limitations to building extensions
- The company responsible for water and sewer
- The connection of property to water mains supply
- Presence of vested water mains
- Basis for charging for water supply

It may be that there are smaller connections not included in the report, in which case you might need to ask for an extended water and drainage search.

As above, your solicitor should summarise the findings for you and highlight the implications.

Environmental Search

Cost: around £50 to £60.

Duration: around 1 to 6 weeks.

This may in summary form be included in the local search and will come separately in more detail if needed. The environmental search looks into environmental factors relevant to you living at the property. This may include some or all of the below:

- Radon gas
- Contaminated land
- Landfill sites
- Industry
- Flooding predictions

- Risk of subsistence

If the summary environmental search reveals no need for concern, you usually won't need a detailed environmental search.

Flood Search

Cost: varies

Duration: varies

A flood search will reveal whether you live in a flood risk area. As mentioned previously in Chapter 4.3, you can check this to an extent yourself. If you already have an environmental search, the flood search should be included.

Extended local search

Cost: around £60 to £80 depending on the provider.

Duration: around 1 to 4 weeks depending on the provider.

This comes under various different names. In essence, your generic local search only looks at issues affecting the property which you are buying. Hence, if you want to know whether planning permissions have been sought for a certain radius around your house, you can often opt for an extended search. You can conduct this yourself by looking through the planning register of your Local Authority, which is typically accessible online. Make sure you know which Ward you are in so that you can see all applications for your Ward. If you request the extended search through the solicitor, you might get some extra information about schools etc included at a price of around £70 to £80.

Chancel Repairs

Cost: around £20.

This is a rudiment from the old days in which homeowners could be made to pay for repairs to the local church by the church. While this seems crazy these days, in some circumstances this right might still stand. Hence, if you are unlucky, you might suddenly be asked to pay for a new altar in your local church. With a change in the law in 2013, this is slowly becoming less relevant. For a similar cost, it is possible to take out chancel repair insurance.

Other searches

Depending where you are buying, you might also do the following searches:

- Coal Mining report. If you live in an area in which coal mining is or was undertaken, you may need a coal mining report to investigate what the impact on your property may be.

- Tin mining searches. As above.

- Check with your solicitor whether any other searches are advisable in your region.

8.3.3 Raising queries: communication between your solicitor and the vendor's solicitor

Once information is retrieved both through the vendor information sheets and searches, it is time for your solicitor to raise queries and sort out legal issues with the vendor's solicitor. This means that formal enquiries will go back and forth between the two solicitors. You can imagine that two lawyers communicating with each other will take ages, and it does.

At this point, it is important that your solicitor 'chases': if no reply has been received to a query for several days, they should follow up. In reality, they will follow up maybe once every two weeks, and this is how delays and wasted time quickly build up. This is where it is important that you stay on top of your solicitor, asking for updates at least once a week and making sure that they follow up on points raised. Imagine the worst case scenario where your solicitor only does work if you really push them. If you only check in with them once per month, they might do nothing in between.

If you are stuck, you can always see whether your agent can help you get your solicitor active by requesting updates. This is in the interest of the agent, as they want to see the purchase go through.

8.3.4 Re-negotiation

If something comes up on the survey or during the due diligence process that you were not aware of and that will result in higher-than-expected costs for you, you can try to renegotiate the price of the property. You can do this via the solicitor, the agent or directly with the vendor. Remember though that the agent will try to get the best deal for the vendor.

If you re-negotiate a relatively small amount, there should be no issues with your mortgage. Just bear in mind that you will have to request an updated mortgage offer, and the contract will have to be re-drawn. This may take weeks, and may not be worth the hassle. Alternatively, you can negotiate that the vendor will fix specified things prior to exchange and/or completion. Then you don't have to change the paperwork, but it's possible that the vendor will do a cheap job or just not do the works after all.

If you re-negotiate a substantial discount – say take £15,000 off after the roof turned out rotten and the electrics unsafe and requiring a full rewire – you have to be aware that your mortgage lender may start to ask questions and updating your mortgage offer may not be so easy. Even if the lender valued the property OK, if you require a large discount due to structural or other problems, your bank may need to re-assess lending on this property.

In either case, it will be sensible to check with your mortgage provider what the terms are for updating a mortgage following a re-negotiation. Also check how long the process will take.

As general guidance, it will be best to negotiate on all aspects of the property that you are aware of BEFORE you agree on your final offer. In the re-negotiation, you can typically only reasonably raise issues that you could not have noticed.

8.3.5 Provisional contract signing and payment of 10% deposit

Once due diligence is complete and all outstanding questions have been answered by the vendor's solicitor, you will get close to the 'real' stuff. This typically starts with your solicitor requesting the following:

- A 10% deposit to be ready for exchange. If you pull out after the exchange of contracts, you will lose this, as the vendor is entitled to keep it plus some compensation.

- A signed, but not dated, contract, ready to be handed over to the other side. Before you do this, triple check it again for all information to be correct. Get someone you trust to check it again for you. This typically requires a 'witness' – someone who will sign confirming that they know you and they witnessed you signing the document. Make sure you have someone lined up to act as the witness for you. If you are buying together, each party needs a witness.

Bear in mind that transferring large amounts of money can take time. Hence, make sure that you initiate the bank transfer 5 days before you want the money to reach your solicitor.

Remember that once you get to exchange of contracts, you are in a binding agreement, and there are repercussions if either party pulls out. The buyer doesn't have much to win from this – if the vendor pulls out, there is only little bits and bobs they may have to pay. If you pull out, you lose 10% of the purchase price and might be asked for further compensation. Have a look at your contract terms before you exchange and make sure you are happy with all arrangements with the vendor. The standard terms which you will likely be signing are here:

https://www.lawsociety.org.uk/support-services/advice/articles/standard-conditions-of-sale/

8.3.6 Communicating with your solicitor

Like it is with all lawyers, solicitors know how to play the game, and you don't. So expect to draw the short straw if there is an issue, even if they caused it. However, there are a few things you can do to at least have a paper trail of communication, agreements, disagreements etc. For a start, make sure you do the following:

- If you write an email, include

  o Request acknowledgement of receipt (you may be able to set a 'read receipt' on your email).

  o Request acknowledgement of any attachments you send (oh yes, that might get overlooked).

- o Be specific what you would like to have answered and what action you request to be taken.

- o Give an indication by when you require the answer to your email.

- If you phone:

  - o Follow up the call in writing (email), summarising what you discussed and agreed.

  - o Include the date and time of the phone call.

- In person:

  - o Summarise the meeting together while you are there.

  - o Draw up action points together while you are there.

  - o Follow up in writing (email) as described for the phone call.

Tips from project management

A little bit of 'project management' will take you a long way. Having a paper trail, or written record, will give you at least some leverage when it comes to resolving problems with your solicitor. If all your agreements were verbally, you can't do anything if they take the stance of "I never said anything". At the same time, if you have a written record, your solicitor should already be aware of any potential holes they are digging for themselves. If you can demonstrate misconduct or poor service based on a record in writing, they will be in trouble with the SRA and Ombudsman should you report them. So you would hope that they pay more attention to written conversations than verbal ones.

When you write to a solicitor, be sure to be super specific and precise. Imagine a 5-year old having to execute on what you'd like. Any room for error, and they might jump on it. Ideally, have someone you trust check and proof-read your written communication and ask them what they understand the instructions to be.

We have found that getting a solicitor to reply – either at all or within 48 hours – can be really tricky to accomplish. Digging around the project management toolbox, we found the following approach to work best:

- Use a subject line similar to this:

  "Action required (today): 40 Brandworth Close"

This makes clear a) they should open it, b) what property the email refers to and c) that they are expected to do something. Be aware that solicitors might get grumpy about being expected to do work and might even try to charge you for a same-day response. Check with their advertising and complain if no satisfactory solution can be found.

- In the mail body, state when you are going to check up on them – they might want you off their back and become active just for that.

- Outline your timelines and logic for them clearly – if you have to get out of a rental by a certain date, make sure they know that and why you have to exchange and complete by a certain time.

- Don't expect them to remember anything you previously discussed or agreed. Always include this as a summary in the mail body to avoid any issues arising from forgetfulness. Refresh important dates, outstanding items and other things that are important. Refresh when you need things to be done by.

8.3.7 More info

- Please refer to the Law Society's Conveyancing Protocol if you want to read more about the conveyancing process and what the buyer's and seller's solicitors should be doing, which you can download it here:

https://www.lawsociety.org.uk/support-services/advice/articles/conveyancing-protocol/

- The standard conditions of sale can be found here:

https://www.lawsociety.org.uk/support-services/advice/articles/standard-conditions-of-sale/

8.3.8 Who can help

Unfortunately, the only person who can help with most problems arising during the conveyancing process is another solicitor. You can also try to manage issues with your solicitor through the head of the office or firm, but the success of this depends on the firm's attitude.

The Solicitors Regulation Authority can help with problems relating to misconduct etc: https://www.sra.org.uk/home/home.page. You can also call them about general enquiries and they will point you in the right direction. The turnaround time for a complaint is around 10 days.

The Financial Ombudsman deals with service-related issues: http://www.financial-ombudsman.org.uk/. The turnaround time is around 8 weeks.

To make a complaint about your solicitor, the Law Society provides good starting information: http://www.lawsociety.org.uk/for-the-public/using-a-solicitor/complaints/

8.4 Survey

8.4.1 Planning ahead

As mentioned previously, make sure you time the survey well. Too early, and you may waste the money on a survey for a property that suddenly stalls. Too late, and you will lose time if your solicitor has to follow up on items and you have to re-negotiate. Too early, and a required re-negotiation may lead to the vendor pulling out and flogging the property to a less critical individual. Too late, and the vendor may not have any scope to re-negotiate, as their onwards purchase has already been set in stone. Stay agile and discuss with your surveyor and solicitor to make sure you do things at the right point in time.

8.4.2 Items investigated in the full survey report

To give you an idea what items the full survey report may cover, here is an example list of the areas reported on:

- Roof coverings and flashings
- Roof spaces
- Chimney stacks
- Boundary walls
- Fascias and soffits
- Rainwater goods

- External pipe work

- External walls

- Damp proof course

- Windows

- External doors

- External decorations

- Internal walls, partitions and ceilings

- Fire places, flues and chimney breasts

- Floors

- Cellar

- Dampness

- Woodboring beetle and rot

- Internal finishes

- Internal joinery

- Sanitary ware

- Services

- Asbestos

- Fire protection and means of escape

- Noise separation

- Grounds and boundaries

- External buildings and conservatories

The outcome of a full building survey should be an approximately 60-page report including images evidencing defects. You have already looked at an example of a Home Buyer's Report (the cheaper and less in-depth option) in Chapter 3.3.3.

8.4.3 Acting on the survey report

Your survey report should have a summary for the following things:

- Matters for the solicitor

- Summary of repairs/actions needed

- Further recommended investigations

Send a copy of the survey report to your solicitor for full consideration. Make sure you spot-check your solicitor – if they are unaware of all items raised in the 'matters for solicitor' section, chances are they haven't looked at the report, despite claiming otherwise.

Discuss these items with your surveyor to decide on the way forward. Price them up and decide which ones you would like to negotiate with the vendor. Decide whether you are willing to take on major repairs – do you fancy replacing a whole roof while being on a full-time NHS job? Do you have the required upfront cash for repairs? Remember, repairs won't come out of your mortgage, you'll have to fork up the cash.

Once you developed an action plan, decide on the way forward with your solicitor.

One thing: it is usually not a good idea to give a copy of the survey report to the agent or vendor. Show them a print copy and let them take a photocopy of relevant pages. If you hand out the whole survey, in worst case it might end up in someone else's hands after you pulled out, and you saved someone else the cost of a survey.

8.5 Other checks

8.5.1 Electrical assessment

In the survey, it may become apparent that the electrics of your property need to be checked. This could be dodgy wiring, a dodgy consumer unit etc. An electrical assessment costs less than a survey, usually around £75 to £200 depending on the depth of the survey, size of the house and number of electrical installations. It may be wise to run this check, as a full re-wire will set you back £3,000 plus potentially thousands of Pounds for re-decoration. At the same time, you shouldn't be careless about electrics. After all, you don't want your new home to go up in flames because the previous owner's dodgy DIY wiring put washing machine, hob and dryer all on the same circuit without fuse. The electrical assessment will include the following checks:

- Summary of the assessment (satisfactory or unsatisfactory)

- Observations and recommendations for actions to be taken

- Electrical supply details and earthing

- Installation at the origin

- Inspection of electrical distribution and circuits

- Circuit details

- Electrical test results

To find a qualified electrician who can carry out an electrical assessment to NICEIC standards, search for a competent person on the NICEIC register here:

https://www.niceic.com/householder/find-a-contractor

Ideally, pick someone who can later do the repairs and whom you get on fine with on the phone.

The outcome of the electrical assessment should be an approximately 13-page NICEIC 'Electrical Installation Condition Report'.

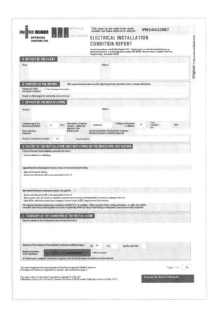

Figure 29. Front page of NICEIC Electrical Installation Condition Report (13 pages at time of writing). ©NICEIC

8.5.2 Gas safety and heating installation assessment

Similar to the above, the survey may bring up that the heating and gas installation should be checked by a qualified gas safety engineer. This takes even less time, and costs accordingly less – plan around £65 to £90 for it.

The gas safety and heating assessment may for example include the following checks:

- Suitability of boiler dimensions

- Safety of all gas installations, including boiler and gas fire

- Any evidence for current or previous leakage of radiators

- State of the heating installation

To find a qualified gas safety engineer who can carry out the assessment, search for a competent person on the gas safety register here:

https://www.gassaferegister.co.uk/find-an-engineer/

As above, ideally pick someone who can later do the repairs and whom you get on with fine on the phone.

8.5.3 Other assessments

Timber and damp survey

If your survey identified damp issues or issues with rot or woodboring beetle, you may require a separate expert timber and damp survey. This will cost around £100, although you might be lucky and get it for free by a specialist company if you are a home owner looking to perform remedial work. This is an important consideration: you have to weigh up the likelihood of the current owners allowing the specialist to lift up their floor against the cost to you having the survey done. If the surveyor has to get through a carpet, laminate flooring and floor boards, chances are the owners will not allow this to happen. The you are stuffed. You need to weigh up the cost to inspection now (around £100) and in future (free for homeowners) against the severity of the potential issue. Your surveyor should have been able to give you context. In worst case scenario, you can make the survey conditional for the purchase or walk away. Be careful not to wind up with a property where the whole ground floor is about to collapse from rot.

Asbestos contamination

If the survey identified potential asbestos contamination and you want material checked further, you can arrange this through a dedicated asbestos specialist. Prices vary depending on the assessment. You can also use online self-testing kits. Just make sure these are run by a legitimate company and are analysed by an accredited lab.

Sulphate attack

If the survey identified a potential sulphate attack risk, you can have a specialist assessment carried out that may cost around £150. Sulphate attack happens when crap underneath your ground floor starts to interact with the concrete of the ground floor, causing it to warp and buckle. It means that your whole ground floor (or the affected area) has to come out and be redone at significant cost and disruption.

Subsistence or Heave

If the survey identified issues with for example subsistence or heave, again you may need to bring in a specialist assessor to establish the causes and risks. Prices vary depending on the assessment.

8.6 Quotes for required works

You may get an initial estimate what works will cost from your surveyor. To get a precise estimate from a builder whom you would like to commission to do the work, you can arrange for the builder to visit the property and give you a quote. Some charge for this – since you ultimately want to compare quotes, this might be a waste of money. Either way, getting a quote from a tradesman capable of carrying out the work will give you peace of mind that your budget is OK. Make sure you get the quote in writing should everything go through and you get them in to do the work. Make sure the quote is valid for a sufficient amount of time to take you past the expected completion date.

If you want additional certainty, get two or three quotes to sanity-check the initial estimate. Just remember that the vendors have to let all these people in and you should ideally be there at the same time. Also, we found that some builders might charge to quote if you don't own whereas quoting for free if you do own. Make sure you don't throw money into the bin.

8.7 Speaking to the vendor

In many people's experience, solicitors are often the road block in the house buying process, causing a lot of stress, anguish and uncertainty for all parties involved. Solicitors have the luxury of going about their business without anyone being able to get a ground truth – unless you speak to the vendor directly.

Based on our own experience, we recommend considering speaking to the vendor directly as early in the process as possible. See whether the agent can arrange a face-to-face meeting in which you can go through questions you may have about the property. See whether the vendor is willing to exchange contact details. Being able to contact the vendor directly may help you a lot, for example:

- You can arrange and confirm any checks directly, such as quotes for works, without waiting days and weeks for the agent to pass information back and forth.

- If your solicitor claims that the process stalled due to lack of reply from the vendor's solicitor, you can check what is going on. You might find the vendor replied ages ago and your solicitor sat on the answer for six weeks.

- If the vendor's solicitor comes back with replies that don't make sense, you can check with the vendor whether it accurately reflects the information which they provided. You may find that the vendor's solicitor answered without consulting the vendors.

- If you are in a chain, you can help each other out trying to get things moving and exchanging information from the chain.

The above of course only works if both, you and the vendor, communicate with best intentions. If you have doubts regarding the vendor's intentions, be careful. Further, make sure that all essential information exchanged informally is confirmed through both solicitors in a follow-up. You can for example agree on a joint statement exchanged between both solicitors.

One thing to be aware of: when you speak to the vendor directly, you might have to manage a lot of emotional and other dramas that solicitors should keep away from you. The vendor might also try to flog you stuff that you don't want and then go on a rampage to destroy everything that he/she can't milk you for. If the situation drifts in any similar direction, it might be best to not communicate any further (or keep it minimal) and ask the solicitor for advice and steer.

8.8 Keeping on top of everything

The conveyancing process is a very stressful period during which you have to make a lot of decisions, haggle, organise a lot of people and keep throwing around a lot of money. To keep on top of everything, keep a log of the following:

- What is going on every day, like a diary of buying your home

- What you are waiting for

- Who is scheduled to do what

- What checks have been done and what actions resulted

The little log book in the appendix will help you with this.

Check in at least once per week with your solicitor to make sure they are working and progressing your case. Get updates in writing and request updates and clarifications in writing – something agreed verbally doesn't count. If your solicitor wastes a month of your rent to inactivity despite agreeing to hit a certain exchange date and then going on holiday, unless you have something in writing, you can't prove anything.

Finally, regularly check in with the agent to get an update on how your vendor is getting on if you are in a chain.

8.9 Exchange of Contracts

8.9.1 What should the solicitor be doing?

Continuing with the Law Society's Conveyancing Protocol, here are the steps that the solicitor should take when acting on behalf of the buyer to prepare and conduct exchange:

Stage D: Exchange of contracts

Exchange

- Discuss your deposit and associated terms with you

- **Exchange contracts**

Post-exchange activities

- Tell you that you need to have buildings insurance cover immediately should you be liable for insurance from the exchange date

- Notify all parties that exchange has taken place

- Obtain and process the 'Completion Information and Undertakings form' (TA13).

- Manage potential Land Registry early completion procedure

- If permitted and required, raise title requisitions

- Prepare stamp duty form with you and prepare its online filing

- Manage transfer specifics

- Prepare and submit an official register search with priority at the Land Registry; also perform bankruptcy checks on you

Managing payments

- Contact the mortgage lender to do the following

  - Send certificate of title and/or requisition of funds. This is the time that your mortgage lender will be asked to send over your mortgage, and when

  - If the advance is sent by CHAPS, request it to be sent one day before completion. Make the request 5 days before the completion date

  - Notify you of potential interest charges after transmission of funds

- Ask you to transfer all your payments related to the purchase (stamp duty, land registry fees) as well as your remaining deposit for the mortgage with sufficient time to clear prior to exchange

In the sections below, we will look at the above in more detail.

8.9.2 Preparation of exchange

Buildings Insurance

Your solicitor should make you aware that you are most likely to be responsible for buildings insurance from the day of exchange of contracts. Make sure you have your quotes to hand and are ready to start insurance cover on the day. In some cases, insurance cover may only be required from the day of completion. Make sure you have in writing which of the two applies.

Check your contract

By now you should have handed a signed, but not dated, contract over to your solicitor. You should already have triple checked that all information on this contract is correct, including your name, the address of the property, the price etc. Still, this might be a good time to glance over them again. Once exchange has taken place, making any amendments will be a pain in the backside.

Agree a completion date

Once all parties involved in the purchase are ready to exchange, they have to agree a completion date. Typically, this is proposed by one party and then communicated up and down the chain (if there is one) or just to the other party. If you are in a chain, this can take days to agree, as everyone's solicitor can delay this and changes in requirements will go back and forth.

It is sensible to communicate your desired completion date early on in the process. Although it has no legal standing, at least it might save you some delays by the time you get to the current stage.

Instruct your solicitor to exchange contracts

When everything is ready, your solicitor will require the final sign-off from you to exchange contracts. It is important to make yourself available during this time, as your solicitor cannot just go ahead and exchange contracts in good faith. Make sure your mobile is charged, sound on and that you check your emails frequently.

Pre-exchange viewing

Now you are only a tiny step away from being bound to buying the house. It is now important to remember that from this point onwards, there is no turning back. The standard terms and conditions of sale stipulate that "**the buyer accepts the property in the physical state it is in at the date of the contract unless the seller is building or converting it**". For this reason, you should do a pre exchange viewing.

During the pre-exchange viewing, verify that everything is as it should be. If you agreed works, these should have been carried out by now. If the vendors still have shed-loads of trash in the garden, it might still be there when you move in. If the house stinks now, it might stink when you move in. If fittings have been broken, they will still be broken when you move in.

If the property has changed and you are not happy about something, discuss it with your solicitor and agent and see whether it can be resolved prior to exchange of contracts. Remember that your estate agent will try to downplay anything you notice, so speak to your solicitor and try to find a solution with the vendor.

If you proceed following the pre-exchange viewing, you have to be absolutely clear that you are willing to accept the worst case scenario – that the property will be as screwed up as it was at the viewing, and possibly more if your vendors live like pigs.

8.9.3 Exchange of contracts

What happens?

This is the big step, and guess what: it's blimmin' archaic! So what happens in theory is that both solicitors meet up and hand over contracts. However, the law has changed and they can now also do it by telephone, and this is what most commonly happens. Your solicitor will hence telephone your vendor's solicitor and read out the contract to make sure contracts are identical. This is called 'release of contracts'. If you are in a chain, this will then go to the next solicitor and so forth until it arrives at the top of the chain. The top of the chain will then start to telephone back down, until the phone of your solicitor rings again. Hence, the process takes time, hours if you are in a chain.

Once your solicitor hears back, that finalises exchange of contracts and you are now only one step away from getting the keys to your new home. You should receive a message from your solicitor confirming that exchange has taken place. Most likely, you will also receive a happy message from your estate agent, who celebrates his/her own commission – errr – would like to congratulate you to your purchase.

Completion information and undertakings form (TA13)

When exchange is taking place, you might receive copy of a TA13 form that specifies how the 'handover' of your new home will take place. This is arranged between solicitors. You can download this form here for your reference:

https://www.lawsociety.org.uk/support-services/documents/TA13-form-specimen/

Importantly, this form guides through agreeing the following:

- Handover of the keys

- Handover of deeds and documents

- How completion will take place

- Transfer of funds

- Mortgage arrangements

Make sure you are happy with how handover of keys and documents is arranged so that there are no hick-ups. You can always ask your solicitor about the points above if you have not been provided with the relevant information.

8.9.4 Things to sort out immediately after exchange

Activate Buildings Insurance

You now have to immediately activate your buildings insurance. You are now liable for the property, and if the current owners burn it down and you don't have it insured, all you got to show for your money is a pile of ashes. Buildings insurance is a compulsory requirement by your mortgage lender, so don't expect to maintain your mortgage on a pile of ashes either. This is REALLY important not to screw up.

If you have taken out buildings insurance with your mortgage lender, they may operate a policy where the insurance is by default active from the date of exchange (maybe even at no cost) and your first payment will come out automatically on the day of completion. In this case, you can lean back and celebrate your easy life.

Activate Life and Critical Illness Insurance

Since you are now liable for the new home, it's time to activate your life and critical illness insurance, unless you are badass enough not to have taken out one. It is likely that at the point of activation you have to confirm a few details, so set aside an hour to sort it out (and retrieve forgotten passwords, just saying...).

Close your Help to Buy account and initiate transfer of bonus

Now it's time to retrieve the fruits of your Help to Buy ISA, should you have one. This requires several steps:

- You need to firstly close the account with your bank. Make sure that before doing so, you print or save the full account statement, as your solicitor might need info on ingoing payments and interest. Once the account is closed, you might lose access to this data.

- Tell your solicitor that you closed the account and that your solicitor should retrieve the funds.

- It might take several days from closing to account to receiving the final account statement, hence allow for this time and discuss timelines with your solicitor. It can be possible that the intent to close the account is sufficient for your solicitor to request the bonus.

- You need to return a First Time Buyer Declaration to your solicitor, which your solicitor should send over to you to fill out. You can find a copy here for reference:

  https://www.helptobuy.gov.uk/documents/2015/12/eligibility-of-ftbs.pdf

...and you can also find loads more information about the process here:

https://www.helptobuy.gov.uk/help-to-buy-isa/further-information/

Release of Mortgage

On exchange of contracts, your solicitor should contact your mortgage lender to release the mortgage funds on a sensible date so that they are available for completion. You should receive notification from your mortgage lender confirming this and giving you the date when the money should hit the solicitor's bank account.

Transfer of remaining deposit

Once contracts are exchanged, your solicitor will need the remaining funds for your deposit ready for completion. Remember, you already paid 10% of the property value, so now you have to 'only' top this up by whatever your total deposit is. As before, allow for a few days for this to leave your account and land on your solicitor's account. You may have to make special requests for large sums depending on whom you bank with. With some banks you may have to pay a fee for transfers over a certain amount, maybe £10,000. What you can of course do is send the money in multiple tranches that stay below such a threshold, as long as your solicitor doesn't freak out about that.

Hand in notice on rental property

The exchange of contracts stage is the safe time to give notice on your rental, if you are housed in one. It might be sensible to do this close to your rental's notice period, so that you don't have new occupants viewing your place for longer than necessary. Have a think about this and check the date on your contract: the 1-month notice period is typically based on the date that you moved in, not the first day of the calendar month. Understand that typically your notice period will be a full month from the date that you moved in:

- If you moved in on the 10th of the month and hand in notice on say the 8th of September, your contract ends on the 9th of October.

- If you moved in on the 10th of the month and hand in notice on say the 15th of September, your contract ends on the 9th of November. Although your landlord may grant you early release if they are nice enough.

You should be able to get specifics of your notice period from your rental contract.

Remember to think about timelines for any required works/repairs now. If you can afford to keep your rental for a few months while you do the new place up, that might be easier to manage. It's up to you.

8.9.5 Your rights

Unfortunately, when you buy a house, the seller has comparatively much more leverage than you after exchange of contracts. While you lose 10% of the purchase price and will be liable for many other costs if you pull out, your rights to compensation if the vendor pulls out are relatively limited.

Your rights are laid out in section 7 of the Standard Conditions of Sale:

https://www.lawsociety.org.uk/support-services/advice/articles/standard-conditions-of-sale/

If the vendor pulls out, you will get your deposit money back (well, you better! This is not really any gain...) and you will be able to get some compensation, but this has to go through the Court. Compensation might for example include deposits for removal companies or temporary accommodation. If the vendor delays the agreed completion, your contract will stipulate the rate at which you will be compensated for. For example, this could be x% of the purchase price *pro rata*. This means that if your house costs £200,000 and you have a 4.5% contract rate, the vendors would have to pay you £9,000 per year and hence around £25 per day for each day of the delay. It ain't gonna make you rich and is unlikely to cover the expenses which will arise for you from the delay. But it's something.

8.10 Completion

8.10.1 What should the solicitor be doing?

Continuing with the Law Society's Conveyancing Protocol, here are the steps that the solicitor should take when acting on behalf of the buyer to prepare and conduct completion:

Stage E: Completion

Completion

- On the day of completion or the day before, manage any delays and related communication with the vendor's solicitor

- If completion by post is performed, manage this based on the Law Society's guidelines

- Update the vendor's solicitor that your full payment of the house is in the system

- **<u>Conduct completion</u>**

Immediately after completion

- Report completion to you

    o   If completion is by post, follow protocol

- Date and complete the mortgage document

- Confirm with you that completion and mortgage went through fine

- Submit the stamp duty return and pay (using the funds you already transferred)

- Submit the stamp duty confirmation to the Land Registry together with the application for registration within the search priority period

8.10.2 Transfer of funds

On the day of completion, your solicitor will gather up all funds (your 10% deposit, remaining deposit payment and your mortgage) and get the money wired across to the vendor. The money takes a slight detour via checking accounts, and hence this can take a moment (as in: hours) to land in its final bank account.

8.10.3 Transfer of keys

Once the money landed in the vendor's account, they should vacate the property (if they have not already done so) and hand over the keys.

The keys can be left with the agent, in which case there has to be an OK from the vendor's solicitor before the agent can pass them over. Alternatively, the keys can be left with the solicitor. Sometimes the vendor might even hand them over in person. Make sure you know in advance where to retrieve the keys from and when. It will be good to look at traffic around that time and general opening hours.

Remember that a lot of completions happen on Fridays. Make sure your solicitor is still in the office if you pick up the keys from there and check how long your agent is open for.

8.11 Post completion

8.11.1 What should the solicitor be doing?

Continuing with the Law Society's Conveyancing Protocol, here are the final steps that the solicitor should take when acting on behalf of the buyer to finish the house buying process:

Stage F: Post-completion

- Apply to the Land Registry in order to remove lendings/mortgages registered against the property using form DS1. You find that form here for your reference:

  https://www.gov.uk/government/publications/mortgage-cancellation-of-entries-for-lenders-ds1

- Manage any delays arising from the vendor's failure to discharge any registered mortgage

  o If there are delays, request a lodgement extension period with the Land Registry in order to avoid the application falling through

- o Inform the mortgage lender of any delays and their reasons
- When the discharge is received under the 'Early Completion' policy and notification of the transfer has been confirmed as received
  - o Check that the contents in the title document are correct. Both you and your solicitor should check this, plus ask someone you trust. Mistakes will cost you. The solicitor is expected to send you a copy of the document for checking.
  - o Confirm updates to the mortgage lender if required
- If there are any issues with registration:
  - o Check all title information again and send you a copy for checking; remind you to keep the 'address for service' up to date
  - o Update mortgage lender on registration completion
  - o Manage all documents and items required by the mortgage lender as per their instructions
- Tell you to keep all your documents safe as you will need them when you come to sell the house on

On the day of completion, your solicitor should notify when your money has arrived with your vendors. You should then get the keys within hours.

It might take a few weeks after you got the keys to receive the final set of documents from your solicitor. Make sure that they communicate timelines with you and keep you up to date.

8.11.2 State of the property

Now that you are equipped with the keys, you can set foot into your very own home. Take it all in.

How the property should be handed over...

Your TA6 form stipulates how the property should be handed over, unless the vendor indicates he/she won't comply with this:

- All rubbish is removed from the property (including from the loft, garden, outbuildings, garages and sheds) and the property will be left in a clean and tidy condition.

- If light fittings are removed, the fittings will be replaced with ceiling rose, flex, bulb holder and bulb.

- Reasonable care will be taken when removing any other fittings or contents.

- Keys to all windows and doors and details of alarm codes will be left at the property or with the estate agent.

Hence, this is how you *should* expect to find the property. Nice and tidy, with all evidence of the previous occupant gone. Also, all fixtures and fittings should still be there as per your paperwork.

...and what you might get

With all of the above in mind, also remember: the standard Terms and Conditions of the sale stipulate that

> *"The buyer accepts the property in the physical state it is in at the date of the contract unless the seller is building or converting it."*

The 'date of the contract' is the date on which you exchanged. The above also translates into the beautiful exemption for anyone who is trying to hide something:

BUYER BEWARE.

It's your problem if you don't detect the flaws – or if you accept them. So the bottom line is: you rely on the vendor having the decency to hand over the property in a nice state. If they don't, there is not much you can do about it other than sue them. And that's no fun:

- If you get the property handed over in a mess, you would have to take steps towards litigation to sort it out. For required works less than £10,000, this would end up in the small claims court. You would most likely have to defend yourself there since solicitors cost a fortune (possibly around £2,500). Plus you have to pay a fee. Whether or not you will have the ruling on your side can be chance level – if the house was a mess at exchange and the vendors promised to sort it but didn't, that might be your bad luck.

- Once your vendor is out, they can pretty much wash their hands of anything to do with the property.

- Your solicitor may not look after you for anything to do with poor state at handover. It is not included in the conveyancing fee. And everyone knows that.

That's why it is so important to properly inspect before committing.

8.11.3 Documents you should receive after completion

Once you got the keys, nothing might happen for a few days or weeks. You should then receive a bundle of paperwork form you solicitor. This should and/or might contain the following:

- Any indemnity insurance certificates / policy for unregistered works

- Any documentation, warranties and logs passed down from the vendors

- The deeds, which are needed to make the application to the land registry; these might be held by your mortgage lender

- SDLT certificate

- Completion of registration documents from HM Land Registry (can take up to 4 weeks)

- Updated title

Chapter 9

Moving in – the first steps

9. MOVING IN – THE FIRST STEPS

This is the point when hopefully the fun will pick up again. You made it! Celebrate and take a deep breath. You completed on your property and now have the keys. This chapter looks at what is likely to come next until you are moved in, so that you can plan ahead for this phase early. We will be looking at the following topics:

- Getting out of your rental accommodation

- Planning repairs and decoration – what should be done before furniture goes in, and what can be done after

- Moving into your new home

9.1 First day at the property

Hurray, it's yours!

Once you got the keys, you can get in. This is super exciting! Your first day at the property might be a complete mix of feelings. You will start to see small flaws that were not obvious. With furniture gone, there may be markings. The owners might have left a mess behind. Well, try not to worry too much about it. Part of the process is to make the home your own, and it can be quite therapeutic to get stuck in tidying. It also makes for fantastic before-after photos.

9.1.1 Being organised on the first day

Stuff to take

We hope you will have a nice first day at your new home. Expect to fix stuff – that's pretty much the first thing everyone does. Before you take off, here is a list of things to take to avoid unlimited runs to the shops:

- Cleaning kit
- Loo roll
- Water/Drinks and Food
- Tea towels and old towels
- Clothes that can get dirty
- DIY Tools
- Measurement tape
- Torch and some kind of extra light if you plan to work after it gets dark
- Notebook and pen
- Bin bags
- Broom, mop and bucket
- Hoover and replacement bags
- (Folding / camping) chairs
- Step ladder

- Kettle

- Phone charger

- Laptop and charger (you can hotspot internet with your phone)

Stuff to check

When you are in, make sure you check the basic functioning of the property:

- Check that the **radiators** turn on.

- Check that the **electrics** work by turning on all the lights. Replace light bulbs where required to make sure the circuits work. Don't touch anything that doesn't look safe.

- Check that the **cold and hot water** work as expected. Check that there are no leaks by looking under sinks, under the bath and everywhere else where you have water connected up while running taps individually.

- Check that the **toilet** flushes and that the **drains** drain.

- Check whether the **boiler** pressure is:

    o Correct (around 1.5 bar cold, around 2.0 bar running the heating system)

    o Stable (that means that the pressure doesn't drop, then you have a leak or something). It doesn't hurt to take a picture of the boiler pressure everyday at the same time when the system is cold. That will reveal any pressure drops.

Don't forget

- **If it is cold/freezing outside, turn the radiators on** and/or put them on timer. You don't want burst pipes on day #2.

- **Document everything**. Take images of everything to have a record of how you received the property. If something is not right and you don't take a picture, you won't have anything to show once you cleaned it up. These images will also help you appreciate the work you put in and to document changes.

- Funny story: the vendor will most likely have taken the washing machine, leaving an uncapped connector. If you are unlucky, that might spew out all the water that comes down your kitchen sink. Check and cap it as required. Same goes for all other **connections that had their utilities removed**.

Leaving the property

This may sound obvious, but when you leave the property behind, make sure all windows are closed and curtains are drawn. Especially, if you started taking boxes full of your things already down there. Nothing is more attractive than ready-packed goods that a thief just has to load on a van. Your neighbours won't know at this stage who is supposed to go in or out, remember.

9.1.2 What if it's not as it should be?

If you receive the property in a state other than agreed in the contract, notify your solicitor and take images of everything that is not OK. You can also try speaking to the agent, although the agent works for the vendor and is unlikely to help you. If you are in communication with the vendor, it might be worth asking what on earth happened and how they would like to put it right. Discuss this with your solicitor first though.

As mentioned above, if the vendor is in breach of contract, you have to take the path of litigation. Have a think how much their mess will cost you and whether it is worth your nerves. From here onwards you would have to go through some court unless an agreement can be found amicably.

As a rule of thumb, expect the property to be in a state that reflects the vendors' attitudes and lifestyles. If they used to live like pigs, they are unlikely to hand the home over deep-cleaned. They might not even have any idea what a clean home looks like and think they did a good job. If they used to run a well organised and tidy household, you should be fine and don't need to expect much trouble.

9.2 Planning repairs and decoration

From the point where you get the keys, you will most likely have a few days, weeks or months until you HAVE to move into your new home. Use this time as best as you can for any repairs that are best done with the house being empty. This includes:

- Work underneath floor boards (e.g. installing radiators).

- Plastering.

- Carpeting and/or laminate.

- Redecoration.

- Any internal structural work.

- Any messy work that creates a lot of dirt which you don't want to clean off your trophy cabinet.

Make sure you allow enough time for these works to complete to save yourself a headache working around a half assembled house full of boxes and furniture.

9.2.1 Sketch out a repair master plan

Once you have a list of repairs, start on the puzzle of sorting them in order of doing them so that you don't ruin with step 2 what you created in step 1. We ended up writing all tasks down, bundling them into work packages either for ourselves or professionals and then sorting them in order of occurrence. We did that by cutting them out and arranging them. For real. Some things can also run in parallel. Make sure that you make the most of any professional working in your house so that you don't have to pay twice for someone to come back. And stack things in order so that they build on one another.

Project Plan – and example

Here is an example: you need to install a new radiator and replace two, install a water supply, have a new electrical consumer unit, need a new power supply to an outbuilding, need new carpet in some of the rooms, have to sort out a few rooms with plaster, want to change the colour scheme of rooms, would like a new carpet on the stairs, need a boiler service, need to re-render the house and fix some stuff on the roof. You start bundling this up as:

1. Plumber / heating engineer (with gas safe registration):

- Install a new radiator and replace two

- Install a water supply

- Boiler service

2. Electrician

- New electrical consumer unit

- Power supply to an outbuilding

- Replace some light switches that turned yellow

3. Carpet fitter

- New carpet in some of the rooms

- New carpet on the stairs

4. Builder / handyman / plasterer

- Plaster rooms

- Re-render the house

5. Painter / DIY

- Change the colour scheme of rooms

6. Roofer

- Fix some stuff on the roof

Next, you put these tasks into logical order, so that each piece of work builds on another. Here, it might be advisable to go in the following order:

1. Start with the fundamentals that will make things messy and need to get into the substance of the home:

- Plumber / heating engineer with gas safe registration

- Electrician

2. Make the best use of people that do separate things – here for example those who can render the inside and outside of the property. The

plasterer can also make good what the electrician might have had to open up, especially when running new wiring under plaster:

- Builder / handyman / plasterer

3. Recycle materials. For rendering you might need scaffolding. If you already pay for that, get the roofing people out to use it at the same time:

- Roofer

4. Once the infrastructure is sorted, you can make it pretty. Now you can go ahead and get the remaining things done without having to rip them out again to fix something else:

- Painter / DIY
- Carpet fitter

As you can see, this needs some careful planning, coordination and consideration for people's availability and timelines. Always leave some buffer between tasks – add something like half to full the anticipated time in case problems crop up or work is delayed.

How long will it take to get it all done?

Everyone underestimates how long things will take, including professionals. Here is what should give you some idea:

- Ask friends who did something similar how long each job took them.
- Ask the professional you are working with for an estimate (in days) how long the job will take them.
- Average all the estimates you can get.
- Add all of the time estimates for sequential tasks up.
- **Multiply by 2** (or 3 if you want to play it super safe)

This estimate should give you enough wiggle room for any unforeseen works and delays. Remember: once you start work on part of the property, more problems will be discovered. You will then need time to fix them, where you will have to wait for someone to become available. Which may then uncover more problems. And so on. Allow yourself plenty of time to deal with this stuff, as most likely you have a working life in parallel.

9.2.2 Builder timelines and quotations

How long does it take to start work?

When starting the renovation project, be aware that most trade people are not available immediately. Here are some rough guidelines what to anticipate:

- A day to a week until a date is available to come and quote from first contact.

- A day to a week (and we have experienced longer) for the person to work out the quote and send it to you.

- A few days (unlikely, unless the job can be done in a few days or something got cancelled) to a few weeks (most likely, especially if work is extensive) to schedule in the actual work and get started.

That's why you should start planning it all out early, aye.

How do I work out whether a quotation is sane?

1. Compare quotes

The best way to figure this out is to compare. Get at least two quotes for the same job. Be specific what the job entails:

- DON'T: "I need 3 new radiators, here, there and there".

- DO: "I need 3 new double-panel, single convector radiators that match the dimensions of the previous ones and integrate with the overall power of the heating system. This should include tidying the connecting pipe work as well as thermostatic valve and lock shield for each new radiator. The system should also be pressure tested and inhibited after installation".

How do you know this detail? You have to cobble it together from online info, DIY manuals and existing quotes.

Make sure the quote is specific about the following things:

- What exact works will be done.

- Whether VAT is included and/or payable.

- How any damages will be handled (for example, when installing windows, making good of the brickwork might not be included).

- What the warranty is.

- How long the quote is valid for.

2. Estimate it yourself

You can figure out at least a rough price by estimating the following costs:

- Time effort.

- Material costs.

So if you need a new boiler, have a look what a new boiler costs. You find a lot of kit on the websites of national companies such as Screwfix, ToolStation and Wickes. Then do some research how long it takes to install it and estimate personnel costs (just for a ballpark figure, take £150 per day). Does it need two people? Then multiply by two. At least that should get you within plus minus 30% of the quotation or so.

3. Use the estimates provided by your surveyor

If you had a good surveyor and agreed on a cost estimate for repairs, that's a solid baseline to work from. They surveyor has no interest in ripping you off and will hopefully have a good idea (and database) what individual repairs cost. Costs might be slightly overestimated to give you a safety margin.

4. Research online

Online can be your good friend. There is tons of information in discussion forums and you can also look at trade websites which may give ballpark figures for the cost of certain repairs.

5. Ask others

Ask people you know who did similar work what they paid. This might be a touchy topic, but will be immensely helpful. You can also ask related tradesmen what another job may cost; e.g. a roofer might have a good idea what re-rendering a facade might cost.

What if the quote is too high?

Negotiate or continue searching. Apparently some builders quote too high if they don't want to do the work. The price should be fair for both sides. If you get a crazy high quote, it might be best to just move on.

If you feel the quote is a bit high, ask for an explanation. Maybe you were unaware of some costs. Maybe the person is trying to mug you off. Always take time to consider the quote and discuss it with friends/family.

Finally, as above, make sure the quote has a full cost break down, else it will be hard to compare. If someone gives you a total figure for ten different jobs and is not willing to break it down, you can't judge how sane it is.

9.2.3 DIY

Naturally, you will be asking: can I do it myself or shall I pay someone? The answer to this will differ for everyone. To help with the decision, the flowchart below might help.

Sound advice irrespective of your capabilities (real or imaginary) is to keep a few things sacred that you let only a trained professional with the right certifications touch. These include:

- Electrics

- Gas

- Structural interventions

Otherwise, you have to weigh up whether a) you have the time (and whether it is worth your time) to do things yourself, b) whether you have the skills and c) whether you can actually do it cheaper, once you factor in the cost of everything you have to buy including tools. Before you embark on DIY, get at least one quote and see whether you can do better.

Obvious tasks for DIY are:

- Painting / decorating

- Replacing and fixing internal doors (fitting them is harder than you think!)

- Laying laminate

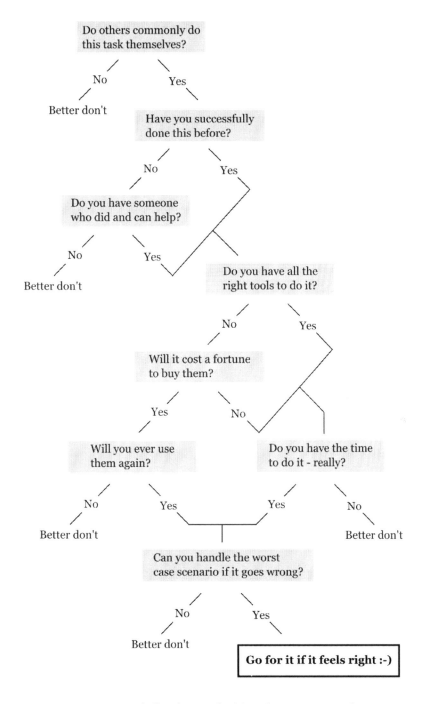

Figure 30. Your very own shall-I-do-DIY decision chart. You are welcome.

So the important consideration for going the DIY route is the total cost of doing things yourself. Yes, you don't have to pay for labour. But how much will it ACTUALLY cost you once you consider the following:

- Cost of new tools.

- Cost of materials (which professionals might get cheaper).

- Loss of holiday allowance or paid leave.

- Cost of putting right your own f*** ups.

Sum this up, compare it to quotes and take it from there.

Naturally, when talking DIY, you will hear a lot from others. Especially parents and grandparents are full of stories of how they fixed up whole houses themselves. Do not get fooled. Memory is a funny thing, and older generations had a lot more training in practical tasks. Do not think that skimming a wall just needs a 10-minute YouTube video and off you go after finishing a few emails. If you do want to put weight on people telling you how easy tasks are, drill down: did they actually do it, or did they just watch a professional do it and it looked "so easy"? When they did it, did it work out first time or how often did they have to do remedial works? Did it cost as little as they thought? Did they get a divorce over it? Make sure you don't get carried away by narrative. DIY ain't easy for most. But it can also be a lot of fun and rewarding – after all, the end product is something you did. If you are interested in psychology, google the 'IKEA effect' – chances are you will absolutely love your slightly wonky DIY job, maybe even more than any perfect job.

9.3 Moving out of rented

Plan the move

You will save on a lot of money and stress if you plan your move in advance. Allow at least two weeks to book, organise and order in all necessary things including:

- Removal company (if desired).

- Any moving van you wish to hire.

- Removal boxes and protection for fragile things.

- Friends and family who may give a hand.

Start packing up things you don't need early, so that you can just shift them across. Make a plan where they should go or where they will be temporarily stored. Try not to move things up and down stairs in your new home more than once just because you have no clue where to put the stuff, it will kill you and your back.

Admin

Don't forget the admin. Things to sort when moving out of rented include:

- Setting up a postal redirection.

- Change your address with all companies that you deal with, including banks, employer and insurances.

- Terminate your contracts:

    o   Phone / Broadband / TV.

    o   Gas and Electricity.

    o   Water.

- Sort out your Council Tax:

    o   Terminate council tax for your rental.

    o   Start council tax for your new place.

    o   Check whether you need to pay anything twice during a transition period.

- Move your insurances across, which may include:

    o   Contents insurance.

    o   Car insurance.

    o   Health insurance.

- Tell the DVLA that your car now lives at a different address (you have to send in your documents for this address change, and you might get fined £1,000 if you don't). Have a look here for more details:

    https://www.gov.uk/tell-dvla-changed-address

- Take your meter readings (photo for evidence) for:

    o   Gas.

    o   Electricity.

- o Water.

Chapter 10

You are not alone. Stories from others

10. YOU ARE NOT ALONE. STORIES FROM OTHERS

Congratulations, you have made it through the whole process. Chances are it was a ride, and you may wonder whether it is just you who encountered all these hurdles and madness. Rest assured – you share the experience with many others. In this chapter, we have compiled a few stories from fellow First Time Buyers. These stories might scare you, or make you laugh, or make you wonder how these things can happen. The important thing is: you are not alone. Every buyer will have their own story that at the time seems insurmountable. Everyone got there in the end.

The stories in this chapter are written by each individual themselves. They were however given the following five guide questions:

- How did you find your home?

- How was your conveyancing process?

- How were exchange and completion?

- How did the moving-in go?

- What do you wish you had known?

Chapter 10 contents

10.1 Stacey

Me and my husband bought a three-storey terraced town house in a semi-rural area that we chose for affordability and a reasonable length of commute to both of our jobs. We did not know anything about how to buy a house and hence had to learn a lot of things the hard way, especially with respect to unexpected repairs once we had moved into the house. Overall, we have loved making the house our home and it is now exactly how we want it to be. We enjoy living there, although issues with the area and neighbours have somewhat dampened the experience.

1. How did you find your home?

Property websites were still in their infancy in 2007, but we did use a mixture of Rightmove and the local estate agents. We spent around 8 months house hunting and looked at around 14 options.

We initially chose a few properties via Rightmove, etc. and arranged visits ourselves. Eventually we went to the local estate agent directly. The agent there advised we should consider visiting a few properties in one day, which she offered to arrange for us. She also showed us around each one of the properties personally. In all, we looked at about 4 or 5 properties, including some that we had overlooked. It was on this occasion that we were shown the house that we ended up buying. We had originally not even considered this house, but when we walked in, it felt right, and we could see ourselves living there straight away. We think that directly comparing several properties and looking at 'wild card' options from the estate agent was a really good way to get a feel for what was right for us.

2. How was your conveyancing process?

Our estate agent was part of a conveyancing network, so they were able to provide everything for us, which included the services of property lawyers. Essentially, call-centre legal advice! It made things a little easier as everything was done over the phone. However, it would have been nice to have dealt with an actual solicitor. Back then we did not look at finding our own solicitor, as we were a bit overwhelmed by the process and did not know how to go about it.

We were expecting this to be quite a clean process as there was no chain either way. Unfortunately, some concern from the conveyancers over the ownership of a small piece of land behind the house slowed the process down while they decided if it would cause us any problems. We didn't really get a resolution to this, although they did allow the exchange to take place eventually. The delay caused by this issue was 6 weeks, and overall the process took 3 months.

3. How were exchange and completion?

As we were first time buyers and the house we were buying had no chain, the exchange and completion were easy. We had 2 weeks between the two and no delays.

4. How did the moving-in go?

While the purchase was going on, we both still lived with our parents.

The house was empty and ready for us to move into on the completion date. We moved in gradually over a period of two months. The first step was to start re-decorating. Once we had enough of the rooms sorted, we started buying things to put in the house, like furniture etc. We managed all this ourselves, using our own car or having items delivered.

Once we'd got somewhere to sleep, we moved in!

5. What do you wish you had known?

- What problems to look for in a property.

We were trying to limit our spending so only paid for the minimum required survey, which I believe at the time was a mortgage valuation. We did not realise then that the mortgage valuation actually does not come back regarding any flaws other than massive structural issues. We had problems with water ingress via the brickwork for several years after moving in, at its peak resulting in waterfalls running down the wall around windows at Christmas. This cost a fortune to diagnose and repair, where several builders installed pricey items such as new windows after misdiagnosing the reason for the problems. Ultimately, it came down to the whole house requiring re-pointing, where there were huge gaps in the mortar between the bricks. A more detailed survey may have revealed this sooner.

- Looking closer at the area.

Over the years, we have witnessed a negative change to our area since we first bought the house and we wish we had examined different areas more closely. Where we live, cuts to council funding has led to council-maintained areas being abandoned and successive creep of antisocial behaviour and trash flying around due to our close proximity to deprived areas. This includes threatening behaviour on cross bikes and criminal activity. One of our direct neighbours turned out to be on the antisocial side as well, which has caused many problems over the years. We wish we had looked closer at the area where we were going to live to avoid such issues.

10.2 Andrew

I bought a semi-detached house just outside of the city I work in, as it was slightly better value than the nearby suburbs. It was my first house, and I had previously lived in a fully-furnished, rented flat. I decided to buy as another increase in rent was on the cards, and I opted for a house because flats tend to be leasehold with exaggerated service charges. I know a lot of people who have bought houses, so got a lot of varied and sometimes contradictory advice. I think that every house and experience is unique. The buying process for me was relatively painless, unfortunately I just haven't been able to settle in. If the rental system in England wasn't so biased towards landlords I would have waited longer before buying somewhere.

1. How did you find your home?

Rightmove was ubiquitous by the time I was looking to buy, so I made lots of appointments through that website. There was one house that I found just by walking past the For Sale sign. It seemed ideal, but on the same day my partner was shortlisted for a job in a different area. I hesitated and missed the opportunity to buy the house. Lots of people since then have asked me why I didn't make an offer. The answer is that I was nervous and naïve in thinking we'd find a house that we'd like as much, which we never did. The one I eventually bought I found on Rightmove. I felt pressured as the rent was probably going to increase to the point that it was cheaper to pay a mortgage. But I've struggled to settle into the home I bought, and often wonder about the house that we missed.

2. How was your conveyancing process?

I did a broad search of solicitors and decided to opt for one local to where I was buying. It was a very small but very experienced firm. The person I dealt with was approachable and sensible, and I had a pretty good gut feeling from the first telephone enquiry. Lots of large firms offered slightly cheaper rates, but I didn't like how I was dealt with during the initial enquiries. It was a risk to go with a relatively unknown, very small firm, but it worked well for me.

3. How were exchange and completion?

Being a first-time buyer, I felt like I held all the cards. If I remember correctly, I think my solicitor recommended that exchange and completion should happen on the same day, so that I was best protected. I think this made the people I was buying off a bit nervous. Plus they had some issues their end, which delayed things a bit, but I wasn't in a rush. I got the impression that the sellers felt a bit frustrated. I initially anticipated that the sale would complete several months before it did, but my more experienced friends told me that it never works like that. In my case they were right.

4. How did the moving-in go?

My tenancy in my flat came to an end a few weeks after the completion date, so I had plenty of time to sort my things in one place and begin decorating the other! One thing I did before moving in was get a builder to have a look. This gave me some peace of mind, but it also proved right what a few people told me: that there's always something wrong with houses. I also had to get furniture for the first time in my life, but by the time my tenancy had ended the house was in a fairly fit state to move in.

5. What do you wish you had known?

Some people told me that they knew which house they wanted as soon as they walked through its front door. The closest time I felt like that was with the house that I missed out on. Unfortunately, I didn't feel that way again, and ended up buying somewhere I've never warmed to. I started to get very nervous leading up to the purchase but thought that I'd settle in eventually. While this may still happen, after more than two years I still don't feel like the house I bought is my home. In my case, this has meant that unexpected problems with the house and area have become exacerbated. As for many others, it was the biggest and most difficult purchase I made, and having a comfortable home is important to me. So, in retrospect it was very silly for me to go for somewhere that I never really felt a connection with in the first place.

10.3 Camilla

My partner and I felt like we were looking for the impossible. After all, we wanted a 3 bedroom house, possibly semi detached, possibly 1930s, definitely with a driveway, a garage and having a garden was a must. We had a limited budget for all we wished for. Hence, it took us a while to find our forever home! We persevered… and eventually found exactly what we wanted. Although needless to say, we had to make a few compromises: firstly on the location, secondly on the state of the property. Eventually we settled on a 4 bedroom 1930s semi-detached house that needed a lot of decorating and renovating a few miles away from our preferred location.

1. How did you find your home?

Finding our forever home was an exciting but challenging process, we must have visited around 30 properties within a 6 months period. At the time, it was 2017, houses within our budget were selling like hot cakes and I found myself a couple of times having to join group viewings. I could not believe it when I went to see a house in Selly Oak and was told by the estate agent there were 30 people viewing that house on just that day!! I did spend 30 minutes every day searching the net and also had email alerts set up with the major online estate agents. Twice, we did find our nearly perfect forever homes but we were outbid. That is when I started looking into less popular websites that only advertised online, some I never even heard of. But it did pay off eventually and that is how we found our forever home, in case you need to know that was via housesimples.com

2. How was your conveyancing process?

I did go for a very reputable conveyancing firm and that was disappointing. I was receiving letters in the post referencing to documents that were not included and there was a major hiccup right at the end of the process.

I had no regular contact unless I was the one proactively chasing them. Being new to the process, I always had to ask for clarification. I wished they would have been a little bit more sympathetic towards first time buyers :-). Most of my dealings were with the paralegal secretary rather than the solicitor assigned to my purchase. This paralegal seemed very disorganised – once, she could not locate some of my papers and I had to re-submit them all. She also never seemed to have any patience nor time to review my questions whenever I called her. On the other hand, I did manage to speak to my solicitor once and she was actually very professional and happy to explain the process in details. I think for us it was mostly the paralegal that made the whole experience disappointing.

3. How were exchange and completion?

Ultimately, the exchange and completion process was quite stressful. This was mainly due to the fact that at 4PM on the day before the exchange, I was advised by a panicky paralegal secretary from the conveyancing firm that £10,000 were missing and were not included in the mortgage fund transfer. I was also told that I had to provide the missing amount asap!! I contacted the bank and was assured that the whole amount was transferred to the conveyancing firm. When I called the firm again and re-iterated that the full amount was transferred, only then the secretary dug deeper and eventually realised she 'misread' what was noted on the transfer document. Needless to say, I was not impressed.

4. How did the moving-in go?

We did not move in straight away, we still kept the house we rented for a further month, we wanted to get a few rooms painted before moving in and also install a new boiler, so we moved stuff in gradually. It was tiring as every weekend was spent packing and moving bits and pieces but worth it as we did not have to sleep with the dust and dirt :-)

5. What do you wish you had known?

- Negotiate the price.

Retrospectively, we should have haggled a bit on the property price. We did offer the asking price for the property on the basis that there were some minor works that needed carrying out and that the vendor was going to undertake these. We did not verify this prior to the exchange of contracts, and we should have, or at least, we should have kept a close leash on progress and asked for updates during the process. In the end, the vendor did not carry out any of the promised works and we had to do them ourselves at our own cost. We in fact loved the house so much we let a few things slip.

- Manage your conveyancer / solicitor.

I would definitely advise to do your research and always be one step ahead when dealing with conveyancing firms, they are not proactive at all and you are the one who needs to ask the questions all the time and double check everything!

- Try out online estate agents.

I would also give the smaller online estate agents a go and not rely solely on the mainstream ones, you might find a few hidden gems :-)

10.4 Sofia

I bought a 1-bedroom leasehold apartment in a lovely part of Birmingham close to work and only a 10 minute drive into the city. I was a first time buyer forced into buying due to problems with a rented flat that had flooded within my first month of being there. The landlords were so slow in sorting the problem, I'd been left homeless and renting had been much more expensive than buying would be. So I decided the only way to having a bit more security was to buy. I had never imagined I would be buying on my own, so I was a little scared at taking on the sole responsibility of a mortgage. With hindsight, it's the best thing I ever did and it's worked out fine. I wish I hadn't been so hesitant and had done it years earlier!

1. How did you find your home?

By accident! I had a day off work to deal with the drama of the flooded rented flat and went for a longer than usual walk to clear my head. I saw a sign for a new development that had a couple of 1 bedroom flats within my budget. Luckily the sales office was open, I viewed the flats available and I instantly fell in love with a grade 2 listed apartment in the location I always wanted to live in! I had seen a few apartments previously and this one pretty much ticked all the boxes as it was newly refurbished, but had lots of character and quirks. It was also close to several parks and walking distance into Moseley village. It really felt like fate had drawn me to the apartment. I spent that same evening thinking about it and it just felt right so I put in an offer the next day, which was accepted. It was at that point the all the real 'fun' started!

Despite meeting all affordability criteria for many mortgage lenders, because the development was new with high eco credentials and there was very little lending history, it meant that all buyers were finding it difficult to secure a mortgage. I had been accepted for a decision in principle with the Halifax but after 2 months they decided they were not going to lend on the development. So I lost a lot of time and had to start all over again, but I found a better deal with Nationwide which actually saved me a decent amount of interest!

2. How was your conveyancing process?

My conveyancer was brilliant, I dealt with her directly and was in constant phone and email contact. She was amazing at keeping in touch and informing me of all the progress and challenges every step of the way. I'd definitely recommend paying a bit extra to avoid the conveyancing warehouses and call centres. I worked for a conveyancing warehouse for 6 months after university so saw the benefits and peace of mind of dealing with one real person. It should have been a straight forward process as there was no chain involved. However, getting to exchange and completion from the first viewing took almost 6 months: 2 months with the mortgage delays and the rest to do with leasehold issues.

3. How were exchange and completion?

As I was homeless during this time, commuting 80 miles to work from my Mum's, staying in hotels and couch surfing when the money ran out, I opted for a simultaneous exchange and completion which worked perfectly for me.

4. How did the moving-in go?

I'd moved myself 3 times in less than 6 months - from a house share to the rented flat, the rented flat to storage then from storage to my own little sanctuary. By that time I had moving down to a fine art and the final time some help from my younger brother as well.

5. What do you wish you had known?

- Mortgage research

Not being afraid of doing your own mortgage research. I started off with a broker but found a much better deal going to the lender direct. Also, with Nationwide if I'd opened a bank account 3 months previously I would have also received preferential rates – research the impact of customer rates and sign up as a customer in advance so that when you are ready to buy you can make the most of the deals lenders have available.

- Mortgage back-up

I wish I had progressed another mortgage option so that I had a back-up ready to go!

- Being less hesitant to buy

Finally, I really do wish I had bought earlier. With hindsight, I could have skipped moving into a rented flat and all the problems and costs that came with it by looking for somewhere to buy. For me, it took the hassle of rental to commit to buying. Now that I have bought, I've got a foot on the property ladder, am building up capital and most importantly the peace of mind of having my own place and that is priceless!

Appendix 1

Glossary

1. GLOSSARY

1.1 Key terms

- **Due diligence:** This is the legal 'detective' work that is conducted to make sure that the home you are buying doesn't throw up any bad surprises. It is actually a pretty straight forward and defined process, it just seems impenetrable at first since lawyers like to speak in tongues. We hope that Chapter 8 will help you understand the process a lot better.

- **Exchange:** The point where due diligence is completed and where you are happy to proceed buying the property. At this point, you enter a legally binding contract and pay 10% of the property value as a deposit, which you will lose if you pull out.

- **Completion:** The point where you get the keys and which triggers release of your mortgage, registration of your title deeds and payment of stamp duty, amongst other things. The property is now yours and you can move in.

- **Stamp Duty:** The tax you have to pay to the government on the purchase price of your property. Check Chapter 2 for details – you may not have to pay any, or you may have to pay a lot.

- **Conveyancer / solicitor:** This is the person/lawyer who manages the legal process of transferring home ownership to you. This person is in charge of the conveyancing process from when you have the offer accepted to when you receive the keys to your home.

- **Surveyor:** This is the person who will inspect your property to assess whether there are any visible or measurable risks with it, such as damp, subsistence, unsafe electrics etc. The surveyor will produce the survey report; you will select the depth of the report, which will cost accordingly.

1.2 Terms that can get confused

Deposit vs. Deposit vs. Deposit

During the conveyancing process and when planning ahead, there will be three things all described as 'deposit':

a) A **10% deposit** you put down at exchange of contracts as a guarantee. You will lose this if you then pull out.

b) A **deposit that supplements your mortgage** to add up to the full house price. This has to be paid at completion. Depending on your circumstances, this may range from 5% to more than 40% of the purchase price.

c) You will be expected to **pay your solicitor a deposit** when you engage them. This should usually be in the region of a few hundred Pounds.

When you talk about deposit, make sure all parties talk about the same thing. Especially if you are on the First Time Buyer equity loan scheme, the 10% exchange deposit may result in a cash flow crisis. Discuss with your mortgage advisor and solicitor.

First Time Buyer vs. First Time Buyer

You will come across the term First Time Buyer a lot, and this status comes with many advantages. However, depending on the context, a First Time Buyer is defined differently:

a) For purposes of **stamp duty and other government First Time Buyer schemes**, the following strict definition applies:

> *"A first time buyer is defined as an individual or individuals who have never owned an interest in a residential property in the United Kingdom or anywhere else in the world and who intends to occupy the property as their main residence."*
>
> Source: gov.uk

b) For purposes of **mortgages**, this definition it typically more relaxed. It describes someone buying their first property even if they have previously inherited, and often even people who have not had a mortgage in a certain number of years. Check the definition with your bank. If you qualify as First Time Buyer, you might get a little bonus payment when you start the mortgage, which always helps. An example of a First Time Buyer definition for mortgages is given for Nationwide below:

"To qualify as a first time buyer your client mustn't have held a mortgage in the last three years (this includes UK and non-UK mortgages)."

Source: Nationwide (as of February 2019)

Term vs. Term

When deciding on a mortgage, you will come across two 'terms':

a) The **mortgage term**, which is the time it will take to pay off the full mortgage. In this book, we try to consistently refer to this as the 'mortgage term' to avoid confusion.

b) The **interest term**, which is the term for the period for which your interest rate is guaranteed. In this book, we try to consistently refer to this as the 'period' to avoid confusion. You are likely to encounter multiple interest terms during the mortgage term: for example, when you opt for a 5-year fixed rate for a 15-year mortgage term, you will renew your interest term at least once during the mortgage term. We know, it's confusing, but you'll get it.

Appendix 2

Your own calculations and wish lists

2. YOUR OWN CALCULATIONS AND WISH LISTS

2.1 What property price can I afford

Item	£
Annual wage (pre-tax)	
The deposit you saved up	
Solicitor cost	-
Survey + Fees	-
Moving, furniture and repairs	-
Stamp Duty	-
Your amount of cash for deposit after costs	
Maximum cost of property at 5% deposit	
What the bank might lend you	
Cost of property* (constrained by _____)	
Your actual minimum required deposit for that (5%)	

2.2 Monthly living and running costs

2.2.1 Your monthly living costs

Item	£ per month
Student loan	
Phone bills	
Internet and TV	
Car maintenance and petrol	
Public transport	
Food	
Clothes	
Medications	
Private pension	
Health- and/or dental insurance	
Travel insurance	
Holidays	
Pets	
Smoking and other addictions	
Hobbies	
Pocket money	
Other:	
Other:	
Total	

2.2.2 Your monthly running costs

Item	£ per month
Buildings insurance	
Contents insurance	
Life and critical illness insurance	
Council tax	
Gas	
Electricity	
Water	
Service Charge	
Parking charge	
Other:	
Other:	
Total	

2.2.3 Total monthly costs

Item	£ per month
Total living costs	
Total running costs	
Other:	
Total	

2.3 Monthly repayments

Item	£ per month
Joint annual wage (pre-tax)	
Joint annual take-home pay	
Joint monthly take-home pay	+
Running and living costs (from previous table)	-
Planned savings	-
Leftover	+
Assumed 10% increase in monthly mortgage repayment for all your leftovers	-
What you could commit to if you go all out	
10% overpayment allowance on your mortgage	
Knowing you can always pay MORE, lower commitment*	
Planned overpayment within 10% margin	

* Approximate figure that would 'feel good'

2.4 Approximating your full mortgage scenario

2.4.1 General scenario

Item	Your estimate
Mortgage amount	
Planned monthly repayment	
Interest rate (long term, e.g. 3.5%)	
Full mortgage repayment term	

2.4.2 Online options

Item	Option #1	Option #2	Option #3
Mortgage term			
Mortgage amount			
Deposit			
LTV			
Period of guaranteed interest arrangement			
Tracker or fixed mortgage?			
Interest rate			
Planned monthly repayments			
Equivalent pay at 10% interest rate			
Remainder left to pay at renewal			
Comments			

2.5 What are you looking for in a home?

Question	Yes	No
How many bedrooms do you want?		
Do you want a big garden?		
Are you prepared to do major work – central heating, electrical wiring, windows, roof?		
Are you prepared to do some work – repointing, repairs, façade rendering, internal decoration		
Do you want a big kitchen?		
Do you want lots of light?		
Do you want a conservatory?		
Do you want a garage and/or off-road parking?		
Are you OK with neighbours?		
Do you want a warranty on your home?		
Do you want good energy efficiency?		
Do you want access to a train station?		
Do you want access to other public transport?		
Do you want to be close to nature or parks?		
Do you want to be close to good schools?		
Are you comfortable living in an area with lots of social housing?		
Other:		
Other:		
What is more important: area or size of the house?		

2.6 Where do you want to live?

Question	Yes	No
Do you want access to a train station?		
Do you want access to other public transport?		
Do you want to be close to nature or parks?		
Are you happy to live next to a busy road or do you want a side street or cul-de-sac?		
Do you want to be close to good schools?		
Are you comfortable living in an area with lots of social housing?		
Do you want to have a short commute?		
Do you need access to the motorway?		
What kind of crime do you not want to be around?		
How close do you want to be to places where you spend time (maybe you take dancing classes, learn to paint, have a regular cooking group)		
Do you want any public offerings, such as pubs, gym, library or shops?		
Other:		
Other:		
What are your no-goes?	• • • • • •	

2.7 Viewing check-list

Item	Note
Age of boiler	
Age of electrics	_____ Rewired? YES/NO
Age of roof	_____ Original? YES/NO
Age of windows	_____ UPVC/Wood?
Structural alterations?	
Condition of...	
External features	
Roof/missing tiles	
Loft, any leaks	
Guttering	
Windows	
Evidence of damp, where?	
Order of internal decoration	
Age and condition of kitchen	
Age and condition of bathroom	
Chain?	
Other notes	
Do you love it? Why?	

2.8 Comparing solicitors

Activity	Option #1	Option #2	Option #3
Legal fees			
Bank transfer charge			
SDLT return			
Checks and documentation			
Land registry fee			
Searches pack			
Other:			
Other:			
Other:			
Other:			
Total			
Location			
Charge if no completion?			
Ratings			
Other comments			

2.9 Additional costs determined during conveyancing

Item discovered	Cost £
Total	

Appendix 3

Conveyancing log book

3. CONVEYANCING LOG-BOOK

3.1 Milestones

Action	Date	Comments
Offer accepted		
Solicitor instructed		
Property off the market		
Mortgage appointment		
Mortgage lender valuation done		
Mortgage offer received		
Contract pack received		
Searches requested		
Searches received		
Surveyor booked		
Survey conducted		

Action	Date	Comments
Survey report received		
Investigations completed		
Cost for all repairs calculated		
Answers to all queries received		
Re-negotiation started*		
Re-negotiation agreed*		
Mortgage offer revised*		
Revised mortgage offer received*		
Contract signed for solicitor		
10% deposit transferred to solicitor		
Home insurance quotes done		
Pre-exchange viewing conducted		

Action	Date	Comments
Exchange date set		
Completion date set		
Exchange of contracts done		
Home insurance policy started		
Help to Buy ISA transferred		
Termination of rental contract		
Completion done – you got they keys!		
Moving planned		
Start date for repairs		
End date for repairs		
Moving in date		
End of rental contract, move out		

3.2 Solicitor action and chase log

Date / time	Contact mode	Details
23/08/18 10:30am	Mail	Requested to chase outstanding queries, which have not been answered for one week

Date / time	Contact mode	Details

Full Contents

Printed in Great Britain
by Amazon